A JOURNEY OF RICHES

Transform Your Wounds into Wisdom

12 Inspiring insights of alchemizing your heart

Published by Motion Media International
Editors: Kit Brookman, Tiffany Oharo, Daniel Decillis, Eric Wyman, Robert Janelle, and Katie Beck.
Cover Design: Motion Media International
Typesetting & Assembly: Motion Media International

Printing: Amazon and Ingram Sparks
Creator: John Spender - Primary Author
Title: *A Journey of Riches - Transform Your Wounds into Wisdom*
ISBN Digital: 978-1-925919-49-3
ISBN Print: 978-1-925919-50-9
Subjects: Motivation, Inspiration

ACKNOWLEDGMENTS

R eading and writing are gifts that very few give to themselves. It is such a powerful way to reflect and gain closure from the past; reading and writing are therapeutic processes. The experience raises one's self-esteem, confidence, and awareness of self.

I learned this when I collated the first book in the *A Journey of Riches* series, which now includes thirty books with over 300 co-authors from over forty different countries. It's difficult to write about your personal experiences, and I honor and respect every author who has collaborated in the series.

For many authors, English is their second language, which is a significant achievement. In creating this anthology of short stories, I have been touched by the generosity, gratitude, and shared energy this experience has given everyone.

The inspiration for A Journey of Riches, Transform Your Wounds into Wisdom was born from my desire to share insights about trauma from a positive perspective. Each chapter is written by a different author sharing their depth of wisdom on have they transformed their wounds.

I want to thank all the authors for entrusting me with their unique memories, encounters, and wisdom. Thank you for sharing and opening the door to your soul so others may learn from your experience. I trust the readers will gain confidence from your successes and wisdom from your failures.

I also want to thank my family. I know you are proud of me, seeing how far I have come from that ten-year-old boy learning how to read and write at a basic level. Big shout out to my Mom, Robert, Dad, Merril; my brother Adam and his daughter Krystal; my sister Hollie, her partner Brian, my nephew Charlie and niece, Heidi;

thank you for your support. Also, kudos to my grandparents, Gran, and Pop, who are alive and well, and Ma and Pa, who now rest in peace. They accept me just the way I am with all my travels and adventures around the world.

Thanks to the team at Motion Media International; you have done an excellent job at editing and collating this book. It was a pleasure working with you on this successful project, and I thank you for your patience in dealing with the changes and adjustments along the way.

Thank you, the reader, for having the courage to look at your life and how you can improve your future in a fast and rapidly changing world.

Thank you again to my fellow co-authors: Dr. Olga Zabora, Joanne Colely, Amita McBride, Catherine Schwark, Lyn Croker, Maria Loper, Cindy Vazquez, Jenny Bot, Bec Bucci, Sonja Anastasia, and Nadia Emalgrabi.

With gratitude,
John Spender

Praise For *A Journey of Riches* Book Series

"The *A Journey of Riches* book series is a great collection of inspiring short stories that will leave you wanting more!"~ Alex Hoffmann, Network Marketing Guru.

"If you are looking for an inspiring read to get you through any change, this is it! This book is comprised of many gripping perspectives from a collection of successful international authors with a tone of wisdom to share." ~ Theera Phetmalaigul, Entrepreneur/Investor.

"*A Journey of Riches* is an empowering series that implements two simple words in overcoming life's struggles.

By diving into the meaning of the words 'problem' and 'challenge,' you will find yourself motivated to believe in the triumph of perseverance. With many different authors from all around the world coming together to share various stories of life's trials, you will find yourself drenched in encouragement to push through even the darkest of battles. The stories are heartfelt personal shares of moving through and transforming challenges into rich life experiences.

The book will move, touch, and inspire your spirit to face and overcome any of life's adversities. It is a truly inspirational read. Thank you for being the kind, open soul you are, John!" ~ Casey Plouffe, Seven Figure Network Marketer.

"A must-read for anyone facing major changes or challenges in life right now. This book will give you the courage to move through any struggle with confidence, grace, and ease." ~ Jo-Anne Irwin, Transformational Coach and Best-Selling Author.

"I have enjoyed the *Journey of Riches* book series. Each person's story is written from the heart, and everyone's journey is different. We all have a story to tell, and John Spender does an amazing job of finding authors and combining their stories into uplifting books." ~ Liz Misner Palmer, Foreign Service Officer.

"A timely read as I'm facing a few challenges right now. I like the various insights from the different authors. This book will inspire you to move through any challenge or change that you are experiencing." ~ David Ostrand, Business Owner.

"I've known John Spender for a while now, and I was blessed with an opportunity to be in book four in the series. I know that you will enjoy this new journey, like the rest of the books in the series. The collection of stories will assist you with making changes, dealing with challenges, and seeing that transformation is possible for your life." ~ Charlie O' Shea, Entrepreneur.

"*A Journey of Riches* series will draw you in and help you dig deep into your soul. These authors have unbelievable life stories of purpose inside of them. John Spender is dedicated to bringing peace, love, and adventure to the world of his readers! Dive into this series, and you will be transformed!" ~ Jeana Matichak, Author of *Finding Peace*.

"Awesome! Truly inspirational! It is amazing what the human spirit can achieve and overcome! Highly recommended!" ~ Fabrice Beliard, Australian Business Coach and Best-Selling Author.

"*A Journey of Riches* Series is a must-read. It is an empowering collection of inspirational and moving stories, full of courage, strength, and heart. Bringing peace and awareness to those lucky enough to read to assist and inspire them on their life journey." ~ Gemma Castiglia, Avalon Healing, Best Selling Author.

"The *A Journey of Riches* book series is an inspirational collection of books that will empower you to take on any challenge or change in life." ~ Kay Newton, Midlife Stress Buster, and Best-Selling Author.

"*A Journey of Riches* book series is an inspiring collection of stories, sharing many different ideas and perspectives on how to overcome challenges, deal with change and make empowering choices in your life. Open the book anywhere and let your mood choose where you need to read. Buy one of the books today; you'll be glad that you did!" ~ Trish Rock, Modern Day Intuitive, Best-Selling Author, Speaker, Psychic & Holistic Coach.

"*A Journey of Riches* is another inspiring read. The authors are from all over the world, and each has a unique perspective to share that will have you thinking differently about your current circumstances in life. An insightful read!" ~ Alexandria Calamel, Success Coach and Best-Selling Author.

"The *A Journey of Riches* book series is a collection of real-life stories, which are truly inspiring and give you the confidence that no matter what you are dealing with in your life, there is a light at the end of the tunnel, and a very bright one at that. Totally empowering!" ~ John Abbott, Freedom Entrepreneur.

"An amazing collection of true stories from individuals who have overcome great changes, and who have transformed their lives and used their experience to uplift, inspire and support others." ~ Carol Williams, Author, Speaker & Coach.

"You can empower yourself from the power within this book that can help awaken the sleeping giant within you. John has a purpose in life to bring inspiring people together to share their wisdom for the benefit of all who venture deep into this book series. If you are looking for inspiration to be someone special, this book can be your guide." ~ Bill Bilwani, Renowned Melbourne Restaurateur.

"In the *A Journey of Riches* series, you will catch the impulse to step up, reconsider and settle for only the very best for yourself and those around you. Penned from the heart and with an unflinching drive to make a difference for the good of all, *A Journey of Riches* series is a must-read." ~ Steve Coleman, author of *Decisions, Decisions! How to Make the Right One Every Time.*

"Do you want to be on top of your game? *A Journey of Riches* is a must-read with breakthrough insights that will help you do just that!" ~ Christopher Chen, Entrepreneur.

"In *A Journey of Riches*, you will find the insight, resources, and tools you need to transform your life. By reading the author's stories, you, too, can be inspired to achieve your greatest accomplishments and what is truly possible for you. Reading this book activates your true potential for transforming your life way beyond what you think is possible. Read it and learn how you, too, can have a magical life." ~ Elaine Mc Guinness, Best Selling Author of *Unleash Your Authentic Self!*

"If you are looking for an inspiring read, look no further than the *A Journey of Riches* book series. The books are an inspiring collection of short stories that will encourage you to embrace life even more. I highly recommend you read one of the books today!" ~ Kara Dono, Doula, Healer, and Best-Selling Author.

"*A Journey of Riches* series is a must-read for anyone seeking to enrich their own lives and gain wisdom through the wonderful stories of personal empowerment & triumphs over life's challenges. I've given several copies to my family, friends, and clients to inspire and support them to step into their greatness. I highly recommend that you read these books, savoring the many 'aha's' and tools you will discover inside." ~ Michele Cempaka, Hypnotherapist, Shaman, Transformational Coach & Reiki Master.

"If you are looking for an inspirational read, look no further than the *A Journey of Riches* book series. The books are an inspiring and educational collection of short stories from the author's soul that will encourage you to embrace life even more. I've even given them to my clients, too, so that their journeys inspire them in life for wealth, health, and everything else in between. I recommend you make it a priority to read one of the books today!" ~ Goro Gupta, Chief Education Officer, Mortgage Terminator, Property Mentor.

"The *A Journey of Riches* book series is filled with real-life short stories of heartfelt tribulations turned into uplifting, self-transformation by the power of the human spirit to overcome adversity. The journeys captured in these books will encourage you to embrace life in a whole new way. I highly recommend reading this inspiring anthology series." ~ Chris Drabenstott, Best Selling Author and Editor.

"There is so much motivational power in the *A Journey of Riches* series!! Each book is a compilation of inspiring, real-life stories by several different authors, which makes the journey feel more relatable and success more attainable. If you are looking for something to move you forward, you'll find it in one (or all) of these books." ~ Cary MacArthur, Personal Empowerment Coach.

"I've been fortunate to write with John Spender, and now, I call him a friend. *A Journey of Riches* book series features real stories that have inspired me and will inspire you. John has a passion for finding amazing people from all over the world, giving the series a global perspective on relevant subject matters." ~ Mike Campbell, Fat Guy Diary, LLC.

"The *A Journey of Riches* series is the reflection of beautiful souls who have discovered the fire within. Each story takes you inside the truth of what truly matters in life. While reading these stories, my heart space expanded to understand that our most significant contribution in this lifetime is to give and receive love. May you also feel inspired as you read this book." ~ Katie Neubaum, Author of *Transformation Calling.*

"*A Journey of Riches* is an inspiring testament that love and gratitude are the secret ingredients to living a happy and fulfilling life. This series is sure to inspire and bless your life in a big way. Truly an inspirational read that is written and created by real people, sharing real-life stories about the power and courage of the human spirit." ~ Jen Valadez, Emotional Intuitive and Best-Selling Author.

TABLE OF CONTENTS

PREFACE

I collated this book and chose authors from around the world to share their experiences about what "*Transform Your Wounds into Wisdom*" meant to them. The eclectic collection of chapters encompasses a myriad of different writing styles and perspectives that embrace the intelligence of our hearts and intuition.

Like all of us, each author has a unique story and insight to share with you. It might so happen that one or more authors have lived through an experience like one in your life. Their words could be just the words you need to read to help you through your challenges and motivate you to continue your chosen path.

Storytelling has been the way humankind has communicated ideas and learning throughout our civilization. While we have become more sophisticated with technology and life in the modern world is now more convenient, there is still much discontent and dissatisfaction. Many people have also moved away from reading books, and they are missing valuable information that can help them move forward in life with a positive outlook. Moving toward the tasks or dreams that scare us breeds confidence in growing towards becoming better versions of ourselves.

I think it is essential to turn off the television, slow down, read, reflect, and take the time to appreciate everything you have in life. Start with an anthology book as they offer a cornucopia of viewpoints relating to a particular theme. Here, it's fear and how others have dealt with it. I think we feel stuck in life or have challenges in a particular area because we see the problem through the same lens that created it. With this compendium and all the books in the *A Journey of Riches* series, you have many writing styles and perspectives that will help you think and see your challenges differently, motivating you to elevate your set of circumstances.

Anthology books are also great because you can start from any chapter and gain valuable insight or a nugget of wisdom without the feeling that you have missed something from the earlier episodes.

I love reading many types of personal development books because learning and personal growth are vital. If you are not learning and growing, well, you're staying the same. Everything in the universe is growing, expanding, and changing. If we are not open to different ideas and a multitude of ways to think and be, then even the most skilled and educated among us can become close-minded.

The concept of this book series is to open you up to diverse ways of perceiving your reality. It is to encourage and give you many avenues of thinking about the same subject. My wish for you is to feel empowered to make a decision that will best suit you in moving forward with your life. As Albert Einstein said, **"We cannot solve problems with the same level of thinking that created them."** With Einstein's words in mind, let your mood pick a chapter, or read from the beginning to the end and be guided to find the answers you seek.

If you feel inspired, we would love an honest review on Amazon. This will help create awareness around this fantastic series of books.

With gratitude,
John Spender

"The place of your pain will become the place of your power."

~ Steven Furtick

CHAPTER ONE

---∽∘⟨✑⟩∘∾---

Healing your Family Wounds
By Dr. Olga Zabora

T his dedication is to my father, my mother, and all of our fathers and mothers. To us children of our ancestors, with gratitude for our lives and the opportunity to heal and learn from our family wounds. May we collect our "Pearls of Wisdom" and restore the flow of energy and love between generations.

As a seasonal psychologist, I share healing techniques that help you restore your wholeness, health, and well-being. This chapter contains three episodes of healing the family wounds that I had to revisit as well as some examples from my clients. In each part, I name those healing techniques to inspire you to heal yourself and know that it can be done.

PART ONE

FATHER

"The Healing Power of Letter"

On a sunny spring day in Los Angeles, I woke up excited – mainly because I was scheduled for a reading with my long-time astrologist, Glenn. My usual reading would be about my chart, transits, soul mission, etc. This time, I decided to try something different and exceptional; thus, I could barely anticipate until the time came for the session. I was counting the minutes until I heard the phone ringing. I asked my astrologist to do the reading about my father this time, who passed away fifteen years ago from a heart attack in his sleep when he was almost forty-five years old. I had this particular need to read because I always had space in my heart, the hole, the wound you could call it, of missing him, and I had the expectation of creating connections and his presence in my life through this reading.

I'm sure that many can relate to the father's wound. Usually, the father is the first man in a woman's life who gives the seed to her mother, who creates and gives birth to a baby. Thus, Mother and Father are symbolically portrayed in fairy tales as a "king" and "queen" and are the first man and woman in the child's world, their role models. Mother is a fairy who magically creates food, and Father is the hero.

In my clinical practice, I have witnessed many stories from my clients about absent fathers, abusive fathers, unavailable fathers, and others. It gave me additional reassurance to share the story about the healing power of writing a letter. I went through my healing journey using different therapeutic modalities to fill this gap of missing my father. Yet, I felt that something was still not there in my life.

My father was a geologist, so I saw him every six months of the year due to his work. But when he returned, he would bring bags full of goodies, including wild strawberries he preserved as well as bags full of pine nuts and so much love. I always remembered him as a big, strong man with a full beard after spending a few months in the wild. I remembered him as a hero. He was *my* hero. When I was six and a half years old, my friend and I got stuck in my building's elevator. We started to panic and scream after the emergency button was silent and realized nobody would rescue us. My father heard us screaming and ran out of the apartment, seeing the elevator door stuck. I saw him quickly rushing to push the doors with his strong torso and moving them inch by inch. He did not know if we were injured or not, and thus, he pushed as hard as he could. I saw how his back was sweating and bruised, with blood appearing on his skin. Finally, the doors opened, and we were freed and saved from this cage. Later that evening, my whole family and many of our neighbors talked about my father being a hero, protecting us. I saw how my mom put the ointment on the scratches and bruises on his shoulders, and I felt so much love and gratitude toward him. Knowing that I was safe and loved, I went to bed, like being wrapped around by loving, muscular arms. I felt protected, happy and proud of my father as a hero.

During the astrology reading, this story was told to remember and honor my father and his energy, to restore and fill in my bottomless hole of missing him in my life. Glenn would only agree to do this reading with a disclaimer: that I was a long-time professional-client and studied astrology before so that we would be on the same page. We looked at the sun and the moon in both of our charts, how they are connected, and how other planets would play out in our lives as if he was alive and we would have our relationship right now, including what discussions we might have. The ninety-minute astrology session flew by, yet, I felt it was insufficient. Glenn suggested to write a letter to my father, and I followed his advice.

That evening, I created the sacred space: I lit the candle and took out the pictures of my father and me together (when we're going on trips, like when he would take me to the zoo when I was a toddler), turned off the cell phone, took out the stack of paper, and started to write the letter. I was writing and crying, laughing and crying again by telling him how much I missed and loved him. And it was grief and loss, love and gratitude. I did this sacred practice for forty days. As you may know, forty days is a holy number in different religions and cultures, where prayers are said, mantras are chanted, and fasting occurs. Transformations happen when a person is taking on austerities (spiritual practice, or sadhana, that purifies the body and mind of the yogi). So, I did this sacred practice every day until that final day when my tears dried out and my heart was filled with light, love, and peace. I felt so much joy and closure that I needed. Then, I put away our pictures, burned all the letters, let the smoke disappear into the night air as it merged with the father sky, and I went to bed feeling safe and secure as if I was that little six-and-a-half-year-old girl whose hero father had saved. Synchronistically, this fortieth day would fall on my father's birthday – the day he would have his sixtieth birthday.

The following day was a Sunday, and I drove towards Capistrano Beach, enjoying the ocean view and spring mountains on the other side of the freeway. On my route, I saw a crystal shop and decided to stop by. The moment I stepped into the store, the woman asked if I wanted to take a picture of my aura (modern computerized Kirlian technology.) I had not done it for a couple of years, so I decided to do it. The moment I put my palm on the sensor, the woman looked at me shockingly and asked, "Did somebody die recently in your family?" I said immediately, "No, not that I am aware of." However, I started to think and then questioned why she asked. Finally, she pointed her finger to the top of the picture, where I would see a white light and a wing shape, and she said: "Angels, here they are." I started to wail and told her about my practice of writing the healing letter to my father for the last forty days and that I had finished it on his birthday. She looked at me with such love and inspiration as she saw the angels around me and said, "Here he is; he is here with you!"

I was in a trance-like state, and the first thing I saw when I opened up the curtain was that the clay medallion was among the other crystals on the table. The blue color was like the pacific ocean with a white angel on it. I stretched my hand toward it, gently held it in my hands, and then flipped it and read: "I am blessed." I paid for the aura picture, medallion, and a few candles and left the crystal shop. I sat in my car, holding this medallion and the photo with white angel wings on top of my head. I felt how my tears of joy, grace, and unconditional love streamed down my face. I felt truly blessed, connected, and loved. I knew he was there with me, protecting me when he was alive with his arms and now with his angel wings. While looking at the medallion, I whispered, "Thank you, Dad. I love you too." I felt complete and confirmed by the power of healing, writing the letter, and synchronicities that always guided me on my life path and healing journey.

Every time I share this magnificent story with my clients or anybody else, they incorporate the writing letter technique in their healing journey. They return to me, reporting the long-lasting healing results, restoring power, love, fulfillment, and grace or closure while grieving their loved ones as I had done. I witnessed the life flow restored, wisdom thrived, and the eyes that were full of life force and gratitude for the love and relationships they had or have now.

This and many other techniques that help us learn our lessons on our healing journey and discover unconditional love and support, I would call "Pearls of Wisdom" in your sacred box. Learn from them, treasure them, and live your joyous life.

PART TWO

MOTHER

"Sacred Return to Divine Mother"

Usually, transformation or changing direction in our lives starts from a "hit" from life: a car accident, divorce, a sudden loss, a serious health diagnosis, and so on. But unfortunately, we are rarely seeking transformation on our own. Instead, we typically get to "push" on to a new level of development by being "forced" to heal our wounds. We still have a choice to hold on to the wound and carry all of our lives and transfer these destructive or unsuccessful habitual patterns onto the next generation. Or, you can face the challenge, your shadow, heal your wound, and be more present in your and your loved ones' lives. Your choice.

It was a beautiful, charming sunny day in Los Angeles, California, in mid-December. I left the beauty salon feeling all made up and pretty with my hair and nails done. I felt on top of the world. I started my car, and just as I was about to change lanes at five miles per hour, I felt a significant impact from the left side: *"Booom!!!!"* I simultaneously hit the left side of my head against the metallic side of my car, then shock, confusion, a feeling of disorientation, and dizziness. At that moment, I didn't realize that it was a concussion. I had never had head trauma before. But that "hit" happened to me, prompting and reminding me that it's another layer to heal and continue my path of healing my mother's wound and my birth trauma triggered by a car accident.

That day, my life path would turn in a different direction toward a healing journey to my deeper self. When I graduated from psychology school, I felt pretty good after finishing the individual therapy course and was sure I was done by then, but this accident made me work harder. I hit the left side of my brain, which governs the right side of the body (masculine) and is associated with logic, reasoning, analytical thinking and math. The right brain is associated with creativity, abstract thinking, and images and governs the left side of the body (feminine). As a result, I was forced to stop my active "male" way of living, my Animus (Masculine) flow of life: achieving goals and being productive to slow down and uncover my Anima (feminine) qualities. Instead of dismissing this part of life, I embraced it, which allowed me to create wholeness in my being, integrating the left and right sides of the brain and balancing male-female polarities.

The concussion I got from that accident steered me from my successful private practice as a highly trained psychologist toward slowing down in life, releasing my caseload until I could perform again due to short-term memory issues and all other concussion symptoms, which took about six months to heal. My therapy style is integrative, and I focus on solutions, seeing through human nature and helping people heal and improve their lives, and creating long-lasting, positive changes. As usual, I, who actively participates in life, had to stay still for three weeks because every step or bend made the blood flow toward my head, and nausea and dizziness immediately flooded me. So, from down to zero-a still point, the journey began.

Of course, my regular yoga practice and hiking were paused, which made me feel even worse, but I knew I had to stay still and heal from the inside. Everything paused in all areas of my life. I felt like a baby in this "regressed state," learning about the world around me. Everything was new, but the difference was that being professional brought anxiety about returning to work and being as efficient as I used to be. Would I be able to lead my exciting life as a psychologist and perform again? Would I be able to survive? This anxiety was similar to how a baby feels anxious and fearful of being removed from its mother–the source of life, love, food and resources. That situation triggered my mother's wound, even though I had worked on my relationship with my mother before. For most of my adult years, I would take care of my mother and my family. This time, I was in a "regressed state," almost like I needed to reinvent myself. First thing's first–to take care of myself. I learned a lot about self-care and self-love by being forced by accident. Otherwise, I would continue to give myself to others to exhaustion. And now, having this wisdom from hard-learned experience, I teach my clients successfully to learn about healthy boundaries and their needs and wants to make progress on individuation and healthy relationships with themselves and others.

As I said, it was a challenging journey at first. When I could walk without dizziness and nausea, I started to search for solutions: the best supplements to restore memory and set up appointments with different healers and practitioners. Unfortunately, physical therapies would not give me my desired result: I wanted to return to where I was before, where I used to function and where I had my sweet spot in life, where I felt most comfortable in my body, mind, and my professional activity. But the worst thing for me was realizing that there was no way back! The world was no longer the same. My memory would not work as it did before. Usually,

I could see ten patients during the day and the next day, write my notes word by word about what had happened during the therapy session. But not anymore. I had to find my way. Every evening before going to sleep, I would ask myself, "Where is me, my usual, comfortable me? Who am I now?" And I would continue to meditate over and over again.

Before returning to my healing profession, I needed to find healing for myself. And now, I had to dive much deeper into exploring the roles we play in our lives as mothers, sisters, daughters, healers, therapists, and others. We are more than that: the roles we play in life. The more I actively searched for healing and answers, the more counterproductive it became. Usually, Holotropic Breathwork would work to release tension in the body or create more profound healing and connection to my inner self. However, not in this situation; I could not strain myself, nor would the yoga asanas or any bending positions work, making me feel worse than ever. Stillness, simplicity, and ease were my best allies at that time for becoming aware of my basic needs and self-love that I very much needed. It was an excellent lesson for me because now I teach my female clients self-love and self-care practices, creating a balance between masculine and feminine energies and a healthy lifestyle during my retreats and breakthrough coaching sessions so that they can integrate it into their lives.

After six months of struggling, I suddenly remembered that a few months before my car accident and the concussion, I went to a Vipassana meditation course for ten days. I again went through this sacred stillness inside me. The Vipassana meditation implies that you silently meditate for up to sixteen hours a day – no writing, phone, internet, or TV distractions – just you and forty other women and men going through a silent journey that Buddha took. We were given the schedule to wake up at four-thirty in the morning and meditate in our room until the gong called us for a nourishing vegetarian breakfast at eight, cooked in silence by assistants who went through the silent practice themselves. On the tenth day, we had Metta Meditation to bless everyone and everything: all-living beings, including yourself. It was a purely rejuvenating and beautiful experience, but I didn't know that I was there for a treat. My joy and happiness were yet to come.

On my way back from Joshua Tree to Los Angeles, I realized my memory had come back! Magically. Oh, my God! I was back. My memory was back. I could feel the freedom to express myself fully and creatively with full power and life force. I touched my "inner self" and connected to the Divine in all of us. I was almost dancing in my car with joy, gratitude, and grace tears! "I am back! I am back to myself!" But I would never be the same, never forget that healing journey, and always honor my inner sacred self! I felt like I was held in the Universe by a Divine Mother. The grace would come my way so that the healing and unconditional love would pour from all the corners of the Universe, from every rock, tree, and person. Oh, Divine Mother! The Nature of the Intelligence inside us. Deep gratitude and love for healing made me even more refined, redefined, deep, and profound. I was driving in this transcendent state for a while. I felt infinite possibilities and being "dissolved" in Mother Goddess's energy – Bhuvaneshwari – one of those Goddesses in Vedic tradition who worships the Divine Mother in her different faces and forms.

Bhuvaneshwari in Sanskrit means "she embraces the cosmos in her whole being." She represents the eternal mother energy as the space containing all that is. Her essence feels like a vast cosmic womb filled with loving, subtle mother energy. Her space allows you to float in her like in the cosmic ocean, like a baby in a human mother's womb. That's how I felt having my refined identity back. I have been seen and held by a loving presence, a compassionate witness of the Divine Mother. During meditation, you can offer her all your anxiety and fear or whatever no longer serves or needs healing. According to Indian tradition, she will take it in, transform and return it to you in the energy of peace. Her spaciousness allows her dissolve everything that needs to be healed. I meditated on her and released my leftover anxiety and fear back to the Divine Mother Bhuvaneshwari, feeling held and embraced in this protective energy. I was back to a loving flow again! It was indeed a miracle of meditation itself!

I actively integrate meditation and mindfulness into my practice with clients during sessions, as homework, and during retreats. I'm creating a safe space for my clients during therapy sessions and sitting as a compassionate witness of their healing journey, the same way as I was witnessed by a gracious presence and was able to heal myself. During this healing process, I was collecting my "Pearls of Wisdom," where I had to learn to be still and care for my body in need, healthily learning self-love and respect. A regular car accident was transformed into a Sacred Journey to my depth. When we transcend our wounds and learn from them, we step into the "Wounded Healer" archetype who can bring wisdom and healing to others as well... Your choice.

PART THREE

CHILD

"Restoring the Joy and Happiness of Your Inner Child"

This car accident and concussion also triggered my birth trauma, even though I had already worked through this trauma and experienced rebirthing with Holotropic Breathwork (Developed by Stan Grof, MD) and Family Constellations Therapy (developed by Bert Hellinger, a German psychotherapist.) These concussion and short-term memory issues made me feel incapable of performing as I used to perform as a highly trained, professional clinical psychologist. As I mentioned earlier, that accident put me in that "regressed state," where I noticed that when I would go to the grocery store, I would have an intense craving for whipped cream or milk. I never had such a strong desire to drink milk, and guess what? I realized that I needed to soothe myself like a baby.

After a few days of drinking milk, I developed an allergic reaction – a skin rash around my mouth and cheeks. It looked terrifying: all red, scabies around my mouth and nose, peeling skin. I had never had skin rashes or allergies before, and honestly, I was devastated. But I knew I had to go through my healing journey and learn from it.

I scheduled a Family Constellations Therapy session again. During the session, while releasing blockages and generational pains, you restore the loving energy flow of life from your ancestors and your parents to you. That way you can connect to them through love, not through pain, developing strength and wisdom to deal with life's challenges, fulfill your mission, your heart desires, and your life as an individual with your full potential.

The most powerful moment was in healing my birth trauma when I was able to soothe my "newborn self" during the active imagination/visualization process: I was able to "see" myself as a newborn baby being taken away from my mom in a birth house (a regular practice then). That newborn baby was scared and fearful to be taken away from the life-giving source and food – Mother! – and away from everything she could be for the newborn child, brought only to be fed a few times a day and again taken away and kept with the other newborn babies in separate rooms. During the visualization process, I gently looked at the newborn baby girl and softly whispered, "You are safe; you are loved. Everything is going to be okay." And I saw how baby-me started to feel calmer and less tense. She looked back into my eyes, and I gently touched her head and continued, "You will see your mom soon; you will survive; you will be fed…." The baby calmed down even more, and I saw how she slowly started to fall asleep. Seeing the smile on her face was such a delightful moment. After that healing session, my cravings for milk disappeared, and I found a NAET practitioner who helped me process and recode my trauma from the accident. As a result, the allergy slowly faded as that fear faded from my whole being. I felt much stronger and more grounded.

Besides Birth Trauma, when newborn babies experience separation from their mothers as soon as they are born, it's hard for them to develop trust in relationships later in life and may have implications for forming a secure attachment. I have seen it in many clients I worked with in my practice, especially when one brings up trust issues or sometimes reports unexplainable fear – visceral fear of being left without resources or abandonment issues-implications of post-birth practices. In this case, we may explore birth trauma in therapy. If appropriate, we carry out this visualization of "soothing the newborn baby" and talking from the adult point of view of someone who grew into a successful CEO of a big financial corporation, a doctor, or other therapists who would come to me in need to heal their birth trauma or other challenges. I see amazing results from these techniques.

The wisdom from my personal experience of the healing journey allows me to be more present during their journeys, help others heal their wounds, and collect their "Pearls of Wisdom"-their learnings. The lessons from life's difficulties are so precious! Would you agree that we grow the most during these challenging times? Just remember: it's not defining you but helping you to find, refine, and redefine yourself, connecting you to your inner healer and wisdom. You, too, can heal and learn to trust the process of life!

Once you have worked through your birth trauma, there is a possibility of revitalizing your Inner Child using visualization or Active Imagination (used in Jungian therapy) to restore joy and creativity, self-assurance and confidence, positive beliefs and expectations, excitement and spontaneity, enthusiasm and spirit of adventure we had as children. We all know that if a child has grown up in less than loving conditions and environment or, even worse, an abusive family, they hide their innermost self using this protective mechanism. Growing up as an adult, a person tends to become less expressive, less trusting, and more analytical, hiding behind the "Persona" facade. They may become locked in the past, still feeling hurt and pain. A negative past life or childhood events may cloud the present, not allowing you to achieve your full potential or become a self-actualized person.

I often ask my clients, "How do you treat yourself in everyday life, especially in times of stress or when you make a mistake? Do you treat yourself with love, kindness, and support, or do you scold yourself for every small mistake you make?" Most of the time, my clients report that they speak to themselves with harsh words, internalizing their parents' or caregivers' diminishing voices. One client said that if she talked to her friend the way she spoke to herself, her best friend would never talk to her again. During sessions, I create a safe healing space where we explore their wounds. I teach my clients to learn how to "re-parent themselves," become a "good enough mother," and learn how to nurture their inner selves, their Inner Child, so that they can live their life fully, joyously, creatively, and happily.

Once people can heal their Father's and Mother's wounds to relieve Birth Trauma and nurture their Inner Child, they can collect their "Pearls of Wisdom" and connect to their loved ones through love, not pain. As a result, we would have happier families, long-lasting marriages, satisfying relationships and friendships, and a healthy community and society overall.

Wishing you all an incredible and liberating healing journey!

"Do not waste your suffering. Pay attention, listen and learn from it."

~ Michael Lewin

CHAPTER TWO

"Who are you?"
Asked the Caterpillar...

By Bec Bucci

D o you ever look back?

Do you?

Do you know what I mean? Look back at your life, stopping and starting the short film clips that make up the whole movie to date. Do you ever watch a particular scene play over and over, hearing a voice saying, "That's not me, that can't be me?" Past lives of incongruent versions of the self that leer back at you in all the grotesque forms, reminding you of the disappointments, the heaviness, and the failed attempts at achieving anything worthwhile. The screaming silence awaits you when you glance into the past and retreat into the formidable truth: yes, that was you. It was all you.

The truth is, I was dying from the inside out like a fly-blown carcass waiting for the maggots to finally spill out. I endured the gut-wrenching pain of living out all those terrible moments over and over again. I was a fraud, a fake, and a phony. A pretend extrovert hiding away her scared, lost little introvert who just wanted someone to love her, sort it out, and make it all better.

Oh, and that was me too, satisfying my need for love in the most desperate ways – unhealthy friendships and lovers. I was blinded by the sweet words and the empty promises until I was completely drained of all emotional and financial resources due to my overwhelming need to experience a real sense of unconditional love. "Somebody, please keep your word, say what you mean and mean what you say." That's all I ever wanted: transparency, love without conditions, and a spot in someone's heart that didn't resemble a mantle for a trophy.

I'm still alive.

I'm still breathing – just.

How did I make it this god damn far?

Trauma changes a person. Like an onion, the layers peel back over a lifetime. Just when you think you have pulled back the last piece – boom! You get served humble pie. "See, you're not as smart as you think." There it is, that voice again, just waiting for the perfect moment to remind you of the things you are not or cannot be. That voice continues to squeal like an overweight, sweaty pig, the filthy trotters of its words dragging through the tendrils of your mind, leaving it stained with untruths that convince you to buy into the avatar's version of itself.

"This is not really who you are," I hear myself say.

Other people's opinions and limitations can cast a dark shadow on the mirror in which we look for our reflection. This symphony of self begins early, even before being born. The unacknowledged memory of DNA coding is playing the notes that form the rhythms of the generations that have come before you; it resonates silently in the background, writing out a future that is yet to be met.

The cold, rough concrete stuck into my skin as I sat on the step outside the Newcastle train station. The white van my father drove was his calling card, along with his loud outbursts and what can only be described as a Jekyll-and-Hyde kind of multiple personality experience. These changes were completely unpredictable and usually accompanied by pacing up and down in short stretches along the carpet or pavement, constantly flicking his fingers through his hair, and all the time mumbling to himself. This particular day was no different, except that I was told to sit and wait, which I did while I watched my father drive away.

Luckily, the train conductor looked a lot like Santa, and seeing as it was so close to Christmas, I must have figured that old Saint Nick was the most logical person to ask for a ride home. Mr. Claus was a man you could trust, after all, a good stranger, and lucky for me this man was trustworthy. It would take three days for the police to identify me after being admitted to the children's hospital, where I arrived only in a nappy. No sweet dress, no cute shoes. Hungry and dehydrated.

I was three years old.

Over the years to follow, I would witness utter horridness. Most memories from that time I do not even dare to share, not from fear of being descriptive, but from a place of renewed power; the control I now have over this beastly biological genealogy that links my cells to such a predatorily abomination.
That is me – all of it.

A freak.

A misfit.

A weirdo.

Those scraps of memory, those short clips of film that seem so unbelievable, are real. Bad shit happens. And it happened to me. I had no choice in the matter, and I didn't volunteer for the experience of childhood trauma that would follow me around like a shadow, leaving me frozen at times. That shadow turned up in all sorts of ways. I hid it behind a happy exterior, but it still crept into the back door. An eating disorder, addiction to exercise, sex, anything to make it go away. That just became a way of life. I was so far down the rabbit hole I didn't even know I was stuck in Wonderland.

At times, I struggled to even contemplate living another day. I was so tired of having to pick myself up over and over again. The rawness of that feeling still hits me in the chest even now. How can it be that the precious gift of life could be given up so quickly? That is the power of trauma that has not been transformed into purpose.

I want to be raw with you. I want to be real in my honest authenticity about the journey back to the light. It was not going to be easy to patch up those gaping wounds with a needle and thread, but I was prepared to pierce through the surface, even with the knowledge that the process of repair was not a skin-deep experience. It was not going to be painless to put myself back together. However, it was absolutely possible.

All of it is me. Every single part, every step on the path, I took it, one foot in front of the other.

It started with a question: why?

Like a nymph, I sat holding my breath just underneath the surface. My fingertips outstretched, touching the fluid surface where sunlight beckoned me to be reborn. What was my purpose? What was all of this for? I could feel the warmth and see how the light trickled down through the water of my life. And that voice spoke once more, only this time it was different. I heard my soul shout for the first time. "RISE!" For the first time in my life, I felt that the growing pains of the past had come to serve me and others. I could hear the voices of my ancestors whispering, "You didn't come this far only to come this far. Fight!." At that moment, when I heard my soul speak through me, I knew I couldn't give up. No, it was my time. Time to become. Time to embrace all the broken parts and make them whole again.

I was a delicate, delicious, and beautiful tapestry of wounds – wounds that would lead me to my freedom so I could be a voice for those who, like me, had forgotten the incredible miracle of being born. My worth was not a reflection of my past or other people's opinions. My worth was simply a reflection of what I had chosen to believe about myself, about my brokenness. A racket, an excuse to sink into normality as a burdened, untransmutable sheep baa-ing away just like the rest of them. Yes, just like the rest of them – I didn't come here to be average. I was here to complete a mission. After all, I had been given a gift. A small box of wisdom about the human condition and ways to connect to the deepest parts of the human soul and shout at the top of the mountain, "You are not done yet."

You know the feeling...

There has to be more...

Right?

What was "I" waiting for?

Of course, there is more, apart from one uncontrollable and unpredictable component that affects everyone. We have no control over it, and we never know how much of it we will get. It's our most valuable commodity, yet our most underrated asset. It is not limitless, promised, or guaranteed. It is here one day and gone the next. If we valued it more deeply than anything else, our behaviors around procrastination, perfection, and progression would be dramatically altered to create an environment that fertilizes growth and cultivates all realms of joy.

Death, of course, is the greatest breakthrough; it's the last chance we have to embrace unpredictability in which the universe completely reveals itself. All of our so-called 'knowing' becomes irrelevant with the revelation that, at this moment, the divine truth will finally be realized. Indeed it is in the unknowing that all truth lies, for true genius demands a symbiotic relationship between the understudied student of life and the great mystery of the void.

Incandescence, the illumination from within, is often stumbled upon when we are forced into a predicament or a situation not of our choosing. Once seen, it cannot be unseen; we stumble across a profound apprehension of the true nature of reality. A meeting in the mirror of the true self is a difficult experience to put into words. It sparks the opening of the satori, and a way of being that can no longer be bandaged by the fantasy.

I fall further into the light. Symbiosis then reveals itself on a much deeper level, exposing the tapeworms in my life that feed on my intestinally digested knowledge, drawing on my exceptionally great internal light and cannibalizing my very soul. The epiphany ignites my rebellion within, one that will challenge that voice, the one that will eradicate the parasites, the one who will access all future relationships for the elements of mutualism. Exploitation will now only occur in a healthy, non-toxic form where the exchange occurs only when each individual is enhancing the chances of survival of self and the other. The illusion lifts like a veil, and I am faced once again with the small cracks that have allowed these parasitic opportunists in. I can no longer escape the silence by pretending to be deaf, as the epiphany has led me to the core of the silence and the attuned inner ear now finds its balance to complete the tightrope walk ahead. I must decide not what I am but what I am not.

Extraction from previous versions of the self is challenging. There will be losses. I mourn them deeply, but I know I can no longer take them with me. I know now that the legacy of my past must become a force for change. For that to occur, I must tenderly fortify the small cracks in my soul to create an impenetrable vessel that can unapologetically exhibit the scars yet still powerfully share the story by showing up each day with something to offer the world. To carry within it an opportunity to make a footprint in time that will resonate far into the future.

No longer afraid of society's judgments, I become the projector, a Queen Bee, and no longer a sheep. I found the deep silence of the wild where freedom rings so loud it becomes an acoustic sound bath floating like a warm summer breeze underneath outstretched wings, creating a thirst for flight. It allows all who have had their wings clipped to experience the royal simplicity of being oneself and being OK with that. To fully step into the whole container of the self and celebrate this gift, this miracle that is you. Yes, you. Like me, you are a miracle, an event so unlikely that it is nearly impossible. You are the representative of "life" that tells the story of an unbroken lineage going back four billion years. Consider that the probability of your father's sperm colliding with your mother's egg is as much a miracle as that of the right ancestors being created that would, in turn, make you. You are "one" in 400 quadrillions. You see, there can be only "one."

Only "one" that can be you.

All of it.

DNA can be transmuted, and fear can be transformed. I know this now. I understand that the universe is a hologram as much as a paradox. The movie of my life was being filmed through a camera with a single critical lens – the same lens I assumed everyone else saw me through. Somehow the version of ourselves that we see in the mirror is brought into being by the thought that the entire universe will perceive us in the same manner as we perceive ourselves—making our whole attachment to imagery and identity completely benign when faced with that moment of the last breath. At that moment, you will wish you had not become a "them" and had embraced the "you." I can speak as an experienced and enlightened survivor of the last breath. I share my journey in the hope that trauma and tragedy are not a precursor to you embracing the opportunity to live fully and experience an extraordinary life.

The first step is to embrace the fear. We are led to believe that there is no gold in the dark, unknown caves. That we should avoid pain at all costs. Most of the time, we have been coached by the fears of others to shut out that which can, in fact, lead to great teachings. By simply shifting perspective to a place of gratitude, fear becomes an opportunity for growth, and we can learn how to disarm that which has kept us frozen.

Now a survivor of complex PTSD, I can personally account for how this turned up in my life. As a child, I lived through detailed descriptions of how my mother would be murdered by carving a hole in the doorframe to insert a gun that would fire just at head level to blow her brains out. These were the ramblings of an unwell individual that nonetheless had a significant impact on my life. I was a child listening with a child's ear that believed this to be a realistic outcome. It terrified me. The many accounts of my father's madness traveled through my childhood like a kaleidoscope of intense anxiety coupled with moments of feeling completely powerless with no rescuer in sight. I had to become that rescuer for myself – we all do. The fight is all yours. The voice now transforms into the stark reality that it does indeed all start with the power of "one," not only with a suit of armor but with a sword forged in the fire of justice made from the metal of undefeatable willpower and a tenacity that can slice open the dormant chrysalis, allowing the warrior wings of the transformed caterpillar to butterfly her way into existence.

It was then at that moment I realized that I was made up of everything "I AM NOT."

I am not broken.

I am not scared.

I am not lost.

I am not fear.

I am not anger.

I am not disappointment.

"I am not alone."

So much energy is given to everything we believe we are. We spend even more energy trying to convince ourselves and the rest of the world of what we think we are. This can mask our growth potential. Being stuck in the egocentric "I AM" can keep you from uncovering and expressing your life purpose. Knowing what "I am not" means that I can be absolutely anything at all. I can even change my mind about it. Today "I am not" a 'chocolate dipped strawberry eating kinda gal' – but who knows what tomorrow will bring? It's this mindset shift that leads you to limitless thinking. I am not defined by all the things I am. This already exists. So if what I am already exists, it does not need replication; instead, it is permitted to evolve. After all, I was not born a tree. If you don't like something, move.

Our language and our thoughts have the power to change everything, especially how you view the power that past wounds hold over you. "I am not afraid." I took off all of my masks, costumes, and dark cloaks to stand naked before the world and say, "Look at my scars." Look at them – love them – as I do. Perfectly imperfect, they are beautiful. They testify to the fact that I was ever here and still remain. When you look at the mended vase, notice that it's stronger than before it was ever broken. It tells a story of courage and bravery, not brokenness. The teachings of overcoming great adversity settle into my humble toolkit, and I am at peace knowing that these gifts will serve me well into the future.

This nakedness, the rawness of being completely exposed, led me to the wisdom of my gifts and the journey of what my life work will be. I first had to immerse myself in honesty; it was time to take ownership of my story while distinguishing the racket from the untrue parts that kept me convinced I was less than capable.

Yes – yes, you are capable, you must simply decide.

And so I did.

I came back up the rabbit hole and bid Wonderland farewell. I took with me only the new identity "Lady Love," a now full-grown woman ready to take on her calling to protect children, encourage women to embrace their whole being and sexual selves, and create a legacy through the power of storytelling. After that, the mission became clear: To do all things with love in mind. It is that simple.

Is what I am doing right now creating more love, love of self, and love within others?

Bee" kind to yourself.

That little girl on the steps of the Newcastle train station is now only a visitor. But, from time to time, she reminds me of just how far I have come and of how much more still needs to be done.

She gave me a voice, a purpose, and my deep conviction to continue to fight for justice in my unique way for those who cannot fight for themselves.

Believe…

…In the impossible

Know that your past does not have to equal your future. That there is a choice. That your future self is begging you to make those choices today that will carve out your desired tomorrow. And remember, there is only one thing we are never assured we will get more of… one uncontrollable and unpredictable component that affects every one of us. It's our most valuable commodity and yet our most underrated asset. It is not limitless, promised, or guaranteed. It is here one day and gone the next.

Isn't it time?

"TO DO YOU."

What are you waiting for?

"Your wound is probably not your fault, but your healing is your responsibility."

~ Denice Frohman

CHAPTER THREE

Healing From a Broken Heart
By Lyn Croker

Introduction

Have you ever had a relationship breakup?

It hurts like hell, doesn't it?

The feeling of having a broken heart.

How do you mend your heart when it's in pieces?

How do you heal when the pain is so intense you can't see yourself coming out the other side?

How do you stop the pain?

You feel like you've put everything into this relationship, given everything of yourself, and it still didn't work.

Having so much pain that you can't ever see yourself dating again.

You may even say, "I'm never dating again," "I'm going to become celibate," or "I'm over men/women," and "I'm not opening myself up to that pain ever again."

You may have even thought they were the ONE, or you saw yourself growing old with this person, so when you finally let your walls down, you're devastated when it falls apart.

Does any of this sound familiar?

I'm here to show you some basic tools and strategies that can help you heal from a broken heart, enabling you to thrive and come out better on the other side.

I'm here to give you hope and to share my story because I'm just like you, I've been through the pain, and I've used these tools and strategies to heal my broken heart and find my soul mate.

It took me 30+ years to learn these strategies and hundreds of thousands of dollars hiring coaches and mentors, doing workshops, seminars, and courses, and now I share this knowledge with you to help you heal, to help you pay it forward, and help others.

My story

I was married for 27 years to my first husband, and I had four wonderful boys with him. When we broke up, it was devastating. I met him when I was 17 years old, and he was my first real love. They say, "you never forget your first love, right?"

I remember the moment I knew it was over as if it was yesterday.

I was unhappy in my marriage for years and was in a lot of turmoil, pain, and confusion. I had four children with this man, so I did everything I could to save this marriage, but I remember the moment when I knew it was over and there was no turning back.

He was in the bath, and I walked in to talk to him about how things were going in our marriage and how I was feeling. It was one of the only times we could get alone time without the kids hearing and interrupting.

Things had been deteriorating for years, and we were growing apart.

I had been doing a lot of self-development/self-discovery and getting to know the real me. When I met my first husband at

17-years-old, I didn't know who I was or what I wanted in life and in a partner.

Over time I realised I wanted to be a better mother, a better wife, a better ME.

I was really proud of myself for how much I had grown and who I was becoming.

All this terrified my husband because I wasn't the same person he had met. He didn't like the changes. He didn't like the person I was becoming. It brought up all his insecurities, but rather than support and encourage me, he resisted.

It was at that moment when he said, "You've changed. I don't like the person you're becoming."

I knew it was over.

There was nothing more I could do to salvage our relationship.

At that moment, the pain was so intense in my chest. It felt like a knife twisting in my heart. It made me gasp and lose my breath for a minute. All my hope of saving this marriage had gone.

It's not just the breakup of the relationship; it's the lost dreams and goals I had, the plans we made together, the realization that it's not forever, and the thought of being a single mum with four children (two now adults).

We often go into a relationship thinking and hoping it will last forever (well, at least I did), especially when we are young and inexperienced in love. So, to have those dreams shattered is devastating.

I didn't want my boys to see me "broken" because I believed I had to be strong for them, and I believed I had to set a good example. When we get knocked down, we get back up.

Little did I know at the time that, oftentimes, the best lessons for our children are the ones where they see you "broken and vulnerable." When they see you dealing with the pain (I learned that lesson later.)

I wanted them to be resilient and have the strength to get back up when they get knocked down because life will knock you down, your heart will get broken, but the heart eventually heals, and we can love again. It doesn't have to be a life sentence.

So, I would curl myself up in the corner of the bedroom, behind closed doors, on the floor, and rock back and forth with the pain, crying so hard there were no more tears left, and cry myself to sleep.

TIP

At the end of the day grief is real. It's the feeling of having lost someone or something you deeply care about, and you need time to heal those inner wounds.

You need to lean into the pain, not run away from it. Some people can't deal with the pain, so they self-medicate with drugs, alcohol, shopping, food, sex, whatever their drug of choice is. This is a temporary fix that often leads to addictions and further prolonged pain.

The last thing I want you to do is to avoid the emotional pain because it sits there waiting to come out, often at the most inappropriate time, like a volcano waiting to explode. So, rather than shutting down and going numb, you need to lean into the pain.

The more you lean into the pain, the quicker you will heal and then move forward in your life.

Another mistake many people make is jumping too quickly into another relationship (there are many reasons why we do this, but that's another book.)

We think that getting into another relationship will heal our hearts, but it doesn't give you time to process the grief or the lessons. Process what went wrong, so you don't make the same mistake in the next relationship.

If we don't learn the lessons, we will often find ourselves in the same position next time around.

Have you noticed the same issues coming up in your next relationship?

Have you seen yourself making the same mistakes and experiencing the same problems/issues in the next partnership?

The realization that I had to make some changes, no matter how difficult, was obvious to me when these same conflicts, these same feelings, were coming up in my subsequent relationships.

I would ask myself, "what's the common denominator here, Lyn?" And, of course, it was ME.

Does this sound familiar?

Most of the time, these issues/problems are patterns/habits that we have unconsciously developed from our childhood, so we bring these same patterns into adulthood and into our relationships.

When we are ready to be honest with ourselves, it gives us back control of ourselves, our behaviors, our thoughts, and our actions. This is so empowering.

Let me give you an example:

My story

My father and brother died when I was very young, so I had a lot of wounds and healing to do around men.

They were the most important men in my life, and when I lost them, I felt abandoned, alone, not worthy of a man's love toward me, and I felt like every man I loved would leave me. Ludicrous thoughts, I know, but when you're a child, we don't know any different.

So, because I didn't heal these inner wounds as a child, when I became an adult and started dating men, my pattern was to push them away when I started to get emotionally involved with them because I was afraid of loving someone, and then they would leave.

I also had control issues because I was afraid of having no control over my relationship, like when I was a child and felt like my life was out of control.

TIP

We all develop patterns/habits from our childhood that we unconsciously carry through to adulthood and into our relationships. The same patterns will be triggered when our partner says or does something.

Most of us have had relationship breakups, and it doesn't matter how long you're together – one year, five years, twenty years, or more. What matters is "how invested were you in this relationship? Did you open yourself up to love again?" Did you open your heart fully to them?

Regardless of being married or not, when you give yourself completely to someone, and that relationship falls apart, it's one of the most painful things you can endure.

When it happens, it's hard to see the other side and be able to love again and open your heart again when it's in pieces.

Plus, the realization of how to divide up material things like finances and assets. Also, more importantly, what do you do about the children and pets?

It's too much to think about when you're in such an emotional state.

Research shows that the brain can't think logically and rationally when it's emotional.

I'm not going to lie to you; it's painful. Life can be painful - but it's in those painful moments that we grow stronger, wiser, and more resilient. Or would you rather prolong the pain and deal with it slowly over years and years? You can't avoid the pain.

It's like pulling off a band-aid. Do you want to pull it off slowly and prolong the pain or rip it off quickly, and it's over in seconds? Your choice.

Learn to embrace the pain.

Learn to look for the positives in the pain.

Learn to look for the lessons in the pain so you don't repeat them.

This can be done. I did it, and you can too. I'm just like you. All it takes is retraining your brain. It's a habit/pattern that can be changed.

The brain is a muscle, and like any muscle, for it to grow stronger, it takes working the muscle and putting it under resistance.

Let me give you an example of what I did to retrain my brain:

My story

So here I am, broken-hearted, a single mother with mortgage to pay, commitments to keep, bills to pay, working a demanding career as a paramedic, two of four boys still to support, and trying to make their lives as stable as possible.

I asked myself, "Do I want to continue to be this unhappy and be an angry mother all the time?"

It was tough. I would put a brave face on (The mask, you know the mask we put on) when around my children, but in the dark, behind closed doors, when the kids were in bed, I would cry myself to sleep, would roll up in a ball and rock myself crying until I had no tears left to cry.

My mind would race one hundred miles an hour thinking of all the negative things, feeling the weight of everything, the heaviness, the pain, and even thoughts of suicide because the pain was so intense I just wanted it to end.

The only thing that stopped me was my children. How could I leave them with that pain, like my father did with me when I was 11 years old? I've had to live with that pain until in my forties. How could I abandon them in their pain? They had already suffered enough. I couldn't add to their pain.

So, I picked myself back up. I put one foot in front of the other. I had to take one day at a time. I've felt this pain before. I knew that the quicker I worked through this pain and leaned into it, the quicker I would heal my wounds, my broken heart.

One day at a time, one moment at a time. I say the Serenity prayer daily: "God grant me the Serenity to accept the things I cannot change, the courage to change the things I can change, and the wisdom to know the difference. Help me take one day at a time and one moment at a time."

Peace always washes over me when I say this. Is there something you say to yourself to help calm yourself or get through tough times?"

Two steps forward…one step back.

I thought about how I would treat my patients or others if it was them going through this. (Often, we are harder on ourselves and can be our own worst enemy, but that's another book.)

So, I eased up on myself. I had to learn to love myself again, or maybe for the first time in my life. (My mirror work helped with this and literally taught me to love myself and feel worthy of great love.)

Click on the link below to see how this one simple exercise can literally change your life like it did mine and many other men and women. (there are four levels to this exercise)

https://www.youtube.com/watch?v=ZTAowVGp3CA&t=4s

Then the anger kicked in (stages of grief). I kept saying to myself, "just feel it, go with it, embrace the stages of grief and pain."

I remember many times still having to function as a paramedic throughout all this, as I had to be empathetic and sympathetic for my patients and still perform my duties to help others in their pain.

I put on the mask, and when we got back to the ambulance station, I would go into the toilet and collapse onto the floor, crying so badly the tears would come out my nose. Then pull myself together for the next emergency call.

Eventually, after feeling the pain, life slowly got easier. The pain wasn't as intense. Eventually, all the self-development work I had done on myself and mindset kicked in.

So many tools and strategies I learned and practiced to this day, every day.

TIP

I performed a burning ceremony where I wrote a letter to my ex-husband and said all the things I wanted to say, expressed all the anger, the pain, the regrets, the mistakes, then I burned it and said, "I release all the negativity, all the pain, all the energy that's been holding me back and will now look forward to the future and better things to come." It helped me release any negative, residual emotions. It was so cathartic.

It was like a weight had been lifted off my shoulders. I felt free; I could see clearly again, and I could hear the birds singing once more.

I was thinking, "what are the positives from this?" (This is a strategy that shows how for every negative experience, there is a positive experience and vice versa.)

What were the lessons from this experience? (There are always lessons, even if you don't see them at the time. That's why you need a coach.)

How can I move forward? (A coach or mentor will help you with this.)

I received some coaching and did some workshops because I knew I needed help to learn from this experience.

You see, we all have blindfolds on when it comes to our own life.

Have you ever noticed how easy it is to see other people's problems and what and how they can get out of their situation, but we can't see our own problems/issues?

That's why we need coaches and mentors. They're able to be on the outside of the problem, looking in when we are on the inside, trying to look out.

Because I wanted to be the best ME that I could be, to have the most amazing relationship, to have the finances I wanted, the lifestyle I wanted, and to have real deep connections with people, I knew I couldn't do this alone.

The definition of insanity is "doing the same thing over and over and expecting a different result."

We need to make changes if we want a different result. The big question is, "what changes?" And that's where mentors and coaches come in.

Over the years, I continued to work on my emotional triggers and my mindset and realized that I needed to change some of my behaviors, thinking, and beliefs.

I wanted to attract my soul mate into my life (That's when I knew I had healed my broken heart, when I'm thinking of opening my heart again.)

Someone I wanted to spend the rest of my life with, someone that gets me, someone that ticks my boxes, someone with who I could be myself (once I knew who I was.)

Many people say to me, "I'd rather be alone because I don't have to make compromises, and I can do what I want to do." While I agree with them, there is another way to look at relationships.

If you are with the wrong person, then yes, it feels like you have to make compromises and can't do what you want to do.

But when you are with the right person, the person that understands you and is on the same page as you, then you don't have to make compromises, and you CAN still do what you want and be yourself.

Everything feels in alignment when you are with your soul mate; everything flows.

Now that doesn't mean you will never have disagreements, but those disagreements are easily negotiated and settled with a WIN-WIN for both of you.

TIP

One of the things I did to attract my soul mate.

I wrote a list of what was important to me and what was not negotiable. Not just physical characteristics but, more

importantly, mental and emotional characteristics. Someone with similar values, belief systems, core needs, and mindset. It didn't have to be the same but had to be similar, in a ballpark radius, so that it wouldn't be a problem in the relationship.

You see, most of us know what we DON'T want in a relationship, but few of us know what we DO want in a relationship because we don't even know ourselves, let alone what we want in a relationship. That's the first step, getting to know ourselves.

In order for me to fully heal, I had to take responsibility for my part in the failure of the marriage. No longer playing the victim and blame game. Because it always takes two, even if the things we did or didn't do were unconscious patterns that we are not even aware of (that's the blindfold.)

Once I did this, it was so freeing. I truly felt free and full of hope, faith, and trust that when I did the work on myself, the universe/ God – whatever you want to call it – had my back because I truly felt worthy of a great partner. My soul mate is working on being the best version of themselves as well, so together we can grow and be the best versions of ourselves.

TIP

So, what seemed like the worst time of my life (the breakup of my marriage) turned out to be the best thing that happened to me.

It gave me the self-confidence to realize "I'm proud of myself" for:

Learning the lessons I had to learn

Embracing the pain and getting to the other side of the tunnel

Getting help

Seeing my blind spots

Healing my inner wounds

Not becoming disillusioned and bitter with relationships

Opening my heart again

Being a good example for my children as they navigate relationships

As I worked on mending my heart, I attracted my soul mate into my life.

It's interesting that my soul mate was there all along, waiting in the shadows until I was ready emotionally, mentally, and spiritually.

I wouldn't have attracted him if I hadn't done the work I needed, the healing of my inner wounds and writing down what was important to me.

Why have a relationship that is average/good/ok when you can have a relationship that is AMAZING/FANTASTIC/AWESOME?

Every day I thank God for bringing Brian into my life. Our relationship is as good as I had hoped and planned it would be.

Do we have disagreements? Of course, we do. Disagreements/ triggers that come up are a way for us to heal more inner wounds we have, so embrace those challenges.

But those challenges are like a "speed hump" in the road, not a "mountain."

Conclusion

Everyone deserves to have their soul mate that adores them, appreciates them, and loves them unconditionally for who they are.

When I did the inner work, my energy changed, and I was ready to attract the right person into my life. After all, how can you expect your partner to be this amazing person if you're not willing to be the same?

Things you need to do to heal your broken heart and find your soul mate:

Grieve- Lean into the emotional pain...

Ask yourself- What lessons do I need to learn from this?

Ask yourself- What do I need to change?

Get help to see your blind spots.

Make changes-heal inner wounds...

Write a list of what you want in your soul mate; values, beliefs, core needs, personality, masculine/feminine energies, love language, mindset.

Be the change - BE the person you want to attract. You can't expect your soul mate to be this person if you're not willing to make changes yourself.

Do a daily practice on self-care.

Do a daily practice on something towards improving your relationship.

If you're not sure where to start in your relationship, download the relationship checklist in my bio to get a better picture of where you need to start.

The most important thing is to take ACTION. Do SOMETHING.

I wish you all the best in your journey of life and hope you find the love and happiness you're searching for.

Remember, relationships don't have to be that hard when you have some basic tools to help you.

"From every wound there is a scar, and every scar tells a story. A story that says, "I survived"."

~ Craig Scott

CHAPTER FOUR

The Journey Within
By Amita McBride

Clutching my chest, anguish pressing through and around every cell of my body, I saw myself falling backward, my body collapsing upon my bed like a limp doll. Then, as I disengaged and floated upwards towards the ceiling, I felt weightless, like an untethered balloon, the moment small hands released it into the sky, as it slowly disappeared from sight.

Nearing the roofline, the air around me began to shift, becoming dense like cake batter. A voice echoed around me with a resounding "No!" and invisible hands began pushing me back toward my lifeless body. Like a deep-sea diver making her way towards the surface for air, the pressure intensifying with each moment, I struggled violently, fighting to stay free.

Re-entry was like landing on a strange planet with no reference point or platform to help me navigate. My body lurched upwards as my heart began to beat once more, and my breath filled my lungs. I began to sob uncontrollably until a tortured sleep took me away.

My heart had stopped of its own accord, broken by a blow of indescribable force with the sudden loss of my beloved only child, my son Sam.

After a lifetime of dedicated and loving service to earth and Spirit and conceiving and bearing my son against some pretty exceptional odds, at that moment, I broke coldly and completely away from Source and everything I loved. I fell from the sky, a balloon imploding from atmospheric pressure and falling helplessly to earth.

No sunlight could reach into my heart. My skin stayed cold even when held within her warmest rays.

My cat and both of my horses, one being my gelding and love of 18 years, also transitioned shortly after my son was taken home. Losing all of my family simultaneously and completely tortured the remaining pieces of me that had any stability within them. What could I possibly have done to receive such horror and punishment from the Universe? The pain was indescribable. Friends of many years told me I was living their greatest nightmare, and they could not bear to see me, their fear choking them. I was adrift at sea in a raging storm, clinging helplessly to a coconut that would soon sink, leaving me to face the wilds alone.

I was born with gifts I didn't understand. From a young age, I was able to tap into the "veil" across this world into the next and "know" and "see" things before they happened. My connection with the earth, plants and Spirit was and is profound and has always been my anchor. Feeling so betrayed and abandoned from the one connection where I felt the deepest trust completely fractured my soul. To add insult to injury, I had dreamed for two years previously that my beloved son would not make it to his 20th birthday. It was terrifying, and it filled me with fear, as my prophetic dreams always came to be. My son is a being of such love, light and gentle beauty; an old, old soul and my twin flame.

For days after being returned to my body, I could hear my son repeatedly saying, "Camino... October... Momma... Please..." Like a record stuck on the same song. It began to drive me to distraction. I couldn't sleep, eat, or function. My entire world had been torn beyond recognition.

I was utterly broken inside. I had no reference point for who I was anymore; I had been a mother for half of my life, carrying love and protective energy for my precious child, who was now gone. I felt completely lost, living in a hell I couldn't escape, even in sleep.

Years before, Elders in South America had shared that a challenging road lay ahead of me. One day I would be given understanding and would see the mosaic of my life, woven with great complexity and beauty, becoming clear to me. They told me I would feel like I was being punished and to remember that that was not the case, to carry within me the knowledge that I had been chosen, as we all are, for certain soul tasks and that this was mine. Soul agreements are made on one level, but walking them here on Earth is another story entirely. The Elders could also see the lightning energy within my body, which amazed me. I had had lightning go through me four times over a few years. They said it represented the four directions. Being selected by the thunder beings for a specific role of service was a great honor as it meant your soul was considered strong enough to take the journey within and survive it.

This didn't inspire confidence, and I asked if I could change my soul agreement. They laughed heartily at my suggestion. When I experienced the lightning go through me, it didn't feel like a blessing. That level of energy moving through you is jarring, intensely painful and recalibrating on a cellular level. It heightened every sensation, sound and color to the extreme. My teeth ached, and the pores of my skin felt the way I imagined the individual quills of a porcupine to feel, each acutely aware of the smallest energy passing by.

I had known for seven years that I would walk the Camino de Santiago, but I could never have imagined under what circumstances this would take place.

I somehow made my way to France in late 2015 and began walking over the Pyrenees Mountains after barely eating or sleeping for weeks, my broken heart taking center stage. Wearing a pack and shoes I had not worn before, the journey within began.

Having grown up hiking and backpacking extensively, one would think that I would be in my element. Yet, being in a state of utter annihilation and exhaustion, I felt no connection to any-thing around me initially. I felt separate and deeply alone. I cared about nothing, not myself or what happened to me. I was there for my son, or so I thought.

All I knew was that I had to walk there on that trail no matter what and begin my journey going into winter. As absurd as that was, considering my state of being, it was all I had, and I held onto it with both hands. I walked for many weeks into late December, continuing past Santiago to Finisterre, the end of the earth, and the ocean.

I walked and breathed, breathed and walked, walked and sobbed, sobbed and walked, at times counting my steps to 100 to begin again and again when I felt incapable of anything else. I repeated mantras, certain that my heart would give out on the trail and leave my body where she lay, merging into the path millions of pilgrims had journeyed upon for a thousand years.

Powerful experiences and profound blessings kept me going against all odds and through all forms of weather: crushing wind and rain, snow and blistering heat, layer after layer of exhaustion and pain, sadness and anguish, and finally, through utter surrender. I walked almost 600 miles across part of France and much of Northern Spain along the path of St Francis, a saint very dear to me. I felt comfort where there were a precious few walking his path of heart.

I pushed myself further into each moment, into each step, each breath pushing me onward. Step by step on this ancient trail. I walked on, preciously held by this sacred Camino, guarded and held by the millions of prayers of so many who had come before.

My beloved son sometimes walked beside me; I could see him and would speak with him as he held my hand across the veil, separated by a single breath. The tattoo etched upon my body in

Gaelic is interwoven with the Celtic Triquetra and bears the words "Twin souls, one heart but a single breath apart." Strangers in small villages welcomed me into their arms, seeing and feeling the pain radiating from my eyes. They reached out to me with such genuine care as I cried and cried.

My son found ways of speaking through others to reach me, as I was so overcome by grief that I couldn't hear him at times. Grandmother Ana, as I call her, looked up at the sky moments after I arrived at her home and told me in Spanish as she began to cry, "Your son, Sam, no, Sammy loves you so much. He is in anguish with the pain you are in, and he is with you." She lit a candle for my son and me for many months, offering me solace in a way I had never known before. An Earth angel, to be sure. My son's presence helped me find the courage to keep going. He continues to send me doves and ravens when I am sad. No language could translate the emotions of my heart, a heart that somehow could keep beating when in thousands of pieces.

It is hard to believe that seven years have passed since then. It feels as though it has been only moments, like clouds crossing over the sun before moving slowly onward. Time stops for nothing and no one. We are born, we die, and everything continues like we were never here. I wanted to scream at the heavens to honor my child. He was honored, but in my anger and despair, I couldn't see it at the time.

I flew to California to place him into the ocean a year later. He loved the ocean. Light spread out over the water as I released him. Above, the clouds changed into the form of a giant angel with wings that stayed for a very, very long time, not moving and witnessed by several people. A raven had led me to this place where he wanted me to let him go. Tears are falling as I write these words, as it's hard to share them. But a gentle presence is urging me forward to help bring comfort, courage and healing to others, to know you are not alone on your own journey within.

All things are in constant transformation, not lost, only changed. These last years have held me in deep contemplation and silence akin to a bear withdrawing into hibernation to rest and regenerate in darkness and quiet solitude. Needing to grieve and curl deeply within myself, I have spun a chrysalis around myself, cradling my being through transmutation and renewal into a completely new life and platform of existence. I am becoming my own butterfly as I no longer dwell in the realm of the caterpillar.

I stepped away from glassblowing – a strong passion – and equine therapy working with children and newly returned soldiers from the ravages of war. I stepped away from my healing work, plants and travel, all that had given me joy and purpose. I was crushed, and everything was a trigger for all I had lost. I couldn't bear to see people with their children or families together or hear laughter. It felt like a dagger plunging into my core every single time. I would walk through a store and see a young man move in a way that would cause me to leave my groceries and flee to my car, where I would be wracked with uncontrollable sobs. I couldn't see how I would ever find a way forward, even with my son's love from afar.

Looking at my journey from where I am now, I can see the mosaic of my life as the cobwebs are cleared away, and the dust is softly blown into the air. My son and I are working together, joining two realms, a bond of immense purpose and meaning.

Nine surgeries to remove scar tissue and adhesions emanating from a complicated delivery until an exceptional surgeon with a disposition both humble and spiritual helped save and repair my sweet body. This connection with a member of my soul family has been remarkable, allowing the space for trust, hope and faith to begin germinating within me. This, combined with a lifetime of layered healing, unexpected blessings, angels and a heart constantly flowing with love, has given me many saving graces.

A problematic family life filled with many hard teachings and much confusion early on has all been part of my soul evolution and journey. Years spent working to understand, grow, learn, forgive and reach gratitude for the lessons that came at a high cost. The dark night of the soul is a powerful and very genuine place to find oneself. Thankfully, there are tiny lights kindled along the way.

Being a lone wolf for much of my life, combined with almost dying many times, emptied all that I thought I knew and who I thought I was until there was nothing left.

I was utterly bled out, an empty shell awaiting a new host. I had a choice to either discover deeper self-reliance and self-love while feeling total vulnerability or give up. I am not a quitter, so I forged onward.

I launched into deep physical healing on a cellular and neural net level to remove all false belief systems, patterns, traumas, fears and untruths, removing myself fully from a platform that had never been mine but one I had adapted to survive. I finally began to step forward, changing behaviors, self-sabotage, emotional traumas, triggers and isolating patterns until the light started to fill me again.

Miraculous changes began to take place. A new network of support appeared as I realized I didn't have to do it all myself. My own history and being a single mother for 12 years had molded me into a singular force that, while powerful, was also exhausting to maintain and very lonely at times. Nor had I known how to truly let my light shine without being ridiculed or feared for the gifts given to me and for carrying a strong energy presence. I continued to hold myself tightly, not allowing myself to be me made me unwell and stifled my being. More time was needed to learn how to be me safely.

I had spent a lifetime putting others before myself, and I did not know how to truly honor myself. Yet as my heart continued to break free of the protective covering I had put in place from a young age, and as my being continued to transform, my cocoon opened, allowing my authentic self to emerge.

Finally, I was able to hear my son once again. Coupled with deep forgiveness with Spirit, with myself and for so many human experiences, I know to the very fiber of my being that I am a united front for the first time in this lifetime.

No matter how alone or exhausting or futile it all has felt at times, some force within me refused to give in – not only for my son but for myself. I have come so far over such treacherous peaks, I refused to believe that the scales would not tip. Dear friends told me to keep going, though they couldn't walk in my shoes. Their honesty, truth, love, and support held me in grace, helping me through some of my darkest hours.

Seeds do most of their transformation underground, where no one witnesses their sacred unfolding. Like a phoenix from the ashes, I was experiencing myself radically changing. How I spoke, carried myself, and felt inside transformed, a quiet dignity holding my center, calmness and peace growing through my inner realm. At the same time, new and authentic friends emerged, with the few true old soul friends still by my side. Deeply rooted relationships are becoming stronger, and my healing practice is becoming clearer and more beautiful, reconnecting me to the path of the heart.

Walking this new platform without my son physically here with me in this world is a daily journey. I am learning a new language every day, or rather, remembering my true language, the language of my heart. She now speaks without fear, knowing I have the courage to listen to her once again and act upon her wise counsel.

What an extraordinary gift to have been a vessel for my son, such a beautiful soul. He still is and always will be my son. Our connection is unbreakable, as is the love we share. There are no promises in this life. But, if we can maintain our center while expanding outward and contracting inward when asked of us, we honor and take care of the precious life given to us for a time.

Just as we are breathed each breath by source, we can rise from the ashes and grow out of the darkness just like the precious seeds, courageous and willing to bring forth new life each season. We are all shaped and molded by all that we encounter and by all that encompasses us, heart and soul.

All of life is a pilgrimage, a Camino taken step by step and breath by breath until it's time for us to leave and go home to begin again. How authentic we are with ourselves is our map guiding us forward. We each must choose if we are the victim or the hero of our story.

May we each have the courage to listen to the voice of our own hearts. There is great beauty even in the midst of the hardest walk. I feel deeply blessed to have been given such special beings in my life. I honor them by continuing forward with all I am, gaining strength when I feel weak by diving intensely into the love we shared and continue to share.

Many years ago, I was "embraced by the earth" in a ceremony where I dug my grave shovelful by shovelful. I prepared for many weeks as though it were my last day on earth. Walking through the seven gateways of life around the fire to lie down within Mother Earth's arms, buried alive overnight with nothing but a small air hole connecting me to breath and life, a profound night took place.

A true death and rebirth forged by my hand. Listening to the drum beat throughout the night, my heartbeat aligned itself with that sacred rhythm. Holding the roots of the grandmother tree, I chose to be next to gave me strength and fortitude during my shamanic freeing of all fears, untruths, and emotional saboteurs. They were sucked out of my body through the air hole and back into the Soul of the World.

The journey within carries us back into the light of truth and knowledge, back into the purest light of our soul. This does not mean we will never feel sadness, anger, or pain, but it moves through us differently. It can't take hold and twist our consciousness into betraying us anymore.

As the sun gently caressed the horizon and I heard the soil being removed from my grave, I emerged into the new dawn just like the tiny seeds cautiously palpating their way into the world of light and sound. As I took my first breaths, I watched a hawk fly high overhead as gratitude and light flowed through my tears. With this new beginning on a beautiful Easter morning, I took the name Amita from the Sanskrit meaning "infinite and immeasurable."

We are all so very powerful beyond what we believe.

May blessings shine upon all of you and all of life everywhere. May we show each other kindness and tenderness as we journey together. We never know when our roles will reverse themselves, when we will be the ones in need of compassion and love-learning how to sink and grow our roots deep into the earth while simultaneously reaching higher and higher with dignity and wisdom like the great grandmother oak tree. We are all a part of the elaborate tapestry weaving and holding all of life within her remarkable story.

"You have to keep breaking your heart until it opens."

~ Rumi

CHAPTER FIVE

Gaining My Wings

By Joanne Colely

O ne day I woke up in more ways than one.

They say you know when it's time. I'd never believed that would ever happen to me because when you live in fear, the thought of escaping is almost too terrifying to contemplate. But as I lay here in the early morning safety of my bed, listening to the waves crashing on the shore from my bedroom window, I knew that time had finally arrived.

The immobilizing fear and foreboding that I usually wake up with, the kind of fear that makes it difficult for me to breathe, has lifted. I don't know why, but today I feel different.

I stretched the sleep from my body as I rolled over to see where the blue of the sky met the blue of the ocean. It's so beautiful out there. I used to love waking up in this room to that view and the sounds of the sea. I built this home believing I would be safe and secure, but those days are long gone.

I pull the bed covers around my shoulders to protect myself from the memories that have carried me into my current reality. But I can't block my thoughts because I know he'll be out there, waiting, beyond the bedroom door. As soon as he knows I'm awake, the torment and cruelty of psychological manipulation will begin – or the endless silence just as it had for so long. Recently, he had driven a knife into our pool table and told me that "next time, it would be my head." This was my wake-up call. My marriage was over.

I didn't want this for myself anymore, and I didn't want this for my two beautiful daughters. They deserved better. It's taken me a long time, but I have finally accepted that nothing will change unless I make it happen. So, the day I thought would never come finally arrived, and I was ready to walk out the door, away from the home I had built; the house I dreamed would be a beautiful haven for my family. But it wasn't to be - my dreams were shattered, and I was frightened of what lay ahead.

I wanted to walk along the beach one last time, so I pulled on my jeans and jumper, and trying not to make a sound, I slipped silently out of the front door and escaped to the beach beyond bare feet.

It felt good to be on the sand and under the blue sky, where a gentle breeze buffeted a few wispy clouds. Out there, I could think clearly; I could plan how I could safely escape with my girls. I knew I had to do this, but it's not exactly what I expected to do in my early 40s.

As children, we are told the tiring mantra, "Sticks and stones may break our bones, but words can never hurt me." Wrong! Words cut deeper than sticks, stones, and even knives. But silence cuts even deeper. Unlike domestic violence, domestic abuse is when the scars are hidden from all to see. The internal wounds I painfully wore, I was told that I put on a very convincing mask back then. The mask was of a successful businesswoman, energetic and happy, and it was one I wore for the world to see. And yet the worse things got, the harder I worked. Looking back now, I see that was my survival mode kicking in.

For many years I was told I couldn't paint. I was no good, so why bother? So I stopped completely. Gaslighting affects your reality, where you question and blame yourself. The worst thing was that I started to believe that I couldn't do anything and that perhaps he was right. But I no longer blame him, as it was my fault for listening! So one day, I stopped listening to his words and took charge of my life by returning to my passion. And if someone had told me I would go on to paint the Prime Minister of Australia, I would have laughed!

Many moments in your life are turning points. People come into your life for specific reasons, either for a brief moment, a few months, years, or a lifetime. I will never forget years before when I had worked as a graphic designer, sharing the same floor as a microwave therapy clinic for people with cancer who had exhausted all other treatments, resorting to this new therapy at the time. I remember sharing an elevator with a gentleman one day, and as the elevator went up, I said, "I'm so glad it's Wednesday; we are on the upward slide to the weekend!" His face grew serious, and as he looked at me intently, he said, "Don't only live for your weekends, don't wish your life away." The doors to the elevator slid open and he stepped out and slowly walked towards the microwave therapy clinic next door to my office. The building had many levels, I didn't know he would go to that level. I had no idea then, but that comment would sit with me for the rest of my life.

During one particularly low period, I decided to throw myself into exercise to block out and avoid my thoughts of self-doubt and worthlessness. I remember one particular day, I decided to do a series of steps created for fitness called Jacob's ladder in Kings Park, Perth. Extremely steep, I sometimes wanted to use my hands to help me climb.

This particular day it was teaming with people from all fitness levels, from regulars to newbies, who threw off their suits to display their Lorna Janes to tackle their daily exercise. (You could always tell who the newbies were by the look of complete shock and horror after just one flight of stairs. They already looked ready to go home, I observed silently smiling to myself.)

After doing a few flights, I grew weary and wondered how I would ever reach the top. On one of the landings on the way up, I abruptly stopped as there was a young man with his trainer resting having a water break. My mouth fell open as I realized this man had no legs. He was climbing this with only his hands! I shook my head and asked if I could shake his hand. He looked shocked, yet his face broke into a huge smile as I said, "I was struggling and whining about how hard this was, yet here you are! What a legend and inspiration!" I then continued to the top of the stairs with a lot more zest and spring to my steps.

Just as I was about to leave for my car, I looked down the stairs once more and the young man was still on the platform, looking up at me with a huge smile. I think I had made his day, but he will never know that he had made mine and I would remember this for years to come.

I blinked and brought myself back into the present. I was enjoying the warm sun on my face when the strangest thing happened. A willy wagtail sat in front of me, wagging its odd tail from side to side. Then, before I could think, it flew and landed on my shoulder! It lingered there a while before flying away, leaving me wondering if 'this little birdy was trying to tell me something.' I later read that a willy wagtail means a fearless warrior. I knew then that I needed to take this as a sign. I needed to stop being a 'worrier' and be a 'warrior.' It was time to transform my life.

I knew I had to find my inner strength and gather my resilience, self-worth, courage and self-belief to pull myself out of this pattern. For years I would make excuses thinking that he would change. But when you think about it, it's hard enough to change yourself! This endless circle kept repeating itself, and I knew he would never stop and only get worse. As Einstein said the definition of insanity is repeatedly doing the same thing and expecting a different result. Something had to change. I don't wish to expand on what happened many years ago, as I feel I need to leave the past. However, the most relevant part of my story is that one day I decided that I deserved better and to start again.

Sometimes, you grow apart over time, and it becomes toxic somewhere along the line. My daughters deserved better than this. By staying, I was showing them that this unhealthy behavior was ok. For years I had thrown myself into work and exercise to block everything out and make myself so 'busy' and 'distracted' that I didn't have the time to think about it. But one day, that didn't work anymore.

So many women like myself feel trapped into thinking they must stay as it's the right thing to do for the kids. But that is just the opposite. Kids aren't silly; they know more than we realize and just want the simplest things. They just wanted to see me happy.

I knew I had to change my life. I thought back on who the old me was. Who am I now? How can I change my life and how can I make it happen? One thing I needed was a plan. I needed to educate myself to find a way. I told my parents that day was hard as I wanted to protect them from this. I grew up in a happy home with my parents and my older brother Mark. My childhood was terrific and my parents were in love. What happened somewhere along the way when I lost my self-worth and thought that I deserved anything less than what I had grown up with?

When I hit a wall, out of pure desperation, I took a short holiday to get away and clear my head with a girlfriend to Phuket. I had sunk into absolute fear and could no longer deny what was happening or stick my head in the sand. So I stayed a few days longer after my friend left and did a boat tour with a group of people. I remember meeting one particular lady that I chatted to at the time and telling her all about my girls. She was a very warm and friendly lady on holiday with her husband and they seemed very much in love.

Our tour visited a cave and once we were inside, a monk sauntered over to me and chose me to beat an ancient gong three times. It was explained that whoever the monk chose could make a wish as they used the gong. I silently surprised myself and wished I would find real true love one day. That evening I was having a quiet meal on the beach when that lovely couple I'd met earlier that day strolled past my hand in hand. He had just put a flower in her hair and she was gazing adoringly at him. Suddenly she noticed me and stopped and immediately sat and took my hand.

What she said next completely took me by surprise. She said, "I strongly feel I need to tell you this. You don't need to tell me, but I know you are unhappy. You only spoke of your lovely daughters today, but not once did you mention your husband. So know that if you stay with him because you think the kids would be happier, you are mistaken. They are much smarter than you may think and only want to see you happy. I know this because this man is my second husband. I now know what real love is and I will never accept anything less." She squeezed my hand encouragingly, winked at me kindly and then continued her walk with her husband along the beach.

I will never forget another life-changing encounter. I was invited to a friend's husband's 40th birthday party. I had experienced an awful day and ended up going to the party alone. I sat in the car for almost half an hour, filled with anxiety over whether or not I should go to the party on my own. In the end, I took a deep breath and thought, this is ridiculous. I am all dressed up and will have a good time.

After arriving at the party, a pretty woman named Kelly, who I had met briefly many years ago, made a beeline to me. She sat me down and looked at me intently, telling me she was a psychic and had a message for me. She saw me in a boat struggling desperately with oars trying to row against the current. She told me to let them go and simply trust the journey I'm meant to be on. My mouth fell open in shock as she described a secret room I had built under my stairs and the door to it was in my kitchen. She also told me that it stored many things and that some old paint equipment was at the very back. She suggested I pull them out and that the second I started to paint, I would make a lot of money and help many people.

What shocked me was that very few people knew that I had painted years ago and also that when I had built my house, I had indeed designed a hidden room under the stairs, because at the time I was a huge Harry Potter fan and I thought my future children would love to play there. It ended up being used for storage for my then mother-in-law and my art equipment was at the back completely unreachable!

The very next day, I pulled it all out and sorted through the paint tubes on my kitchen bench. My daughter had a new friend over that day, and when her mum picked her up, she saw all of my paints spread out on my kitchen bench that I was sorting and then also noticed the paintings I had done on the walls. She thoughtfully looked at them for a moment and then spun around abruptly and asked rather excitedly if I could teach her daughters how to paint. I had never taught before, but I said yes. How could I say no? This was yet another major turning point.

Her girls loved it and wanted to continue learning, and word started to spread. I began to teach art to kids on weekends to make extra money to enable me to take my girls to the movies or buy their Christmas and birthday presents. My pay covered the mortgage and living expenses with no child support or extra financial help, but nothing was left over for savings or treating my girls. This money gave me a sense of freedom. The joy it gave me to see the difference I was making to these kids inspired me to, later on, make a huge career change and teach art to kids. Many of the children I taught were bullied or had behavioral issues. I empowered them and built up their self-confidence through my creative teaching while always playing classical music to enhance their skills.

It was nearing my 40th birthday and my parents both knew that my dream had always been to celebrate it in Paris. So they pulled me aside and insisted that I go overseas with a couple of girlfriends for a few days and that they would take care of my girls. Unable to afford a trip to Paris, a special deal appeared before me online that was affordable. A few nights in Singapore, including universal studios and one night at the famous Marina Bay Sands with the infinity pool I had always dreamed of swimming in! So before I knew it, I was on the plane with two girlfriends for an exciting new adventure!

I had stayed off social media for a few months, but I had decided to hop back on and share a few pictures of our fun holiday. A few minutes later, not long after I had shared some pics, an old friend of mine from art school contacted me to ask if we could catch up! It had been 22 years since I had seen this friend so I thought, why not? Taking a photo of our reunion, not long after, a few other mutual friends back in Perth that I had also studied with were impressed that we had caught up and wanted me to see them upon my return! I told them I would love to catch up and come to the Merrywells at the Perth Crown Casino, not to bring any 'presents' but to bring their "'presence.'" One friend asked if he could get another old friend of mine along that wasn't on social media and would be in Perth that particular night (as he was usually away, being a FlyInFlyOut worker.)

Remembering him very well from all those years ago, I, of course, said yes. Not long after my return from Singapore, I discovered that I had won a Facebook competition, where I had to give a reason why I should win a $1000 dress. My winning answer was that I was a single mum about to turn 40 and that I only owned corporate suits or active wear but would love to look fabulous on my birthday! So the night of my birthday celebrations, I had chosen to celebrate it on the 11th. The number 11 was my very special lucky number; though I didn't realize it at the time, this night would be a night that would change my life forever.

I will never forget this moment for the rest of my life. The second I looked at Kian, I knew he would never leave my side. Tall, olive skin dressed immaculately, his exotic Persian chiseled looks and commanding presence made my eyes grow wide as his intense sparkling eyes slowly looked me up and down. The electricity I felt the second our eyes locked was indescribable. I hadn't seen Kian for more than 22 years since art school (he was the now FIFO worker who, by pure chance and luck - or fate - happened to be in Perth this particular night.) But as his gaze slowly looked me up and down (I'm so glad I won that dress competition,) I felt drawn to him like our souls were always meant to be. He never left my side that night and still hasn't from that very day. We married on the 11th of the 11th, a few years later. Because of his constant fierce belief in me, my life began to change dramatically.

I attended a Women's International Day Luncheon one year after we were together. A courageous woman called Julie Adams got on stage and told her amazing story. She had worked in nursing for many years and experienced extreme bullying from her peers. Not only that, but she was also experiencing domestic abuse at home. Her husband left her and suddenly, she became a single mum to her three children. Not knowing where to turn, she fell into a deep depression, staying in the darkness of her parent's spare room for three months. After these dark times, she emerged with a business idea. She loved her job as a nurse and wanted to make changes for her patients, so she came up with Chemo@Home. This business soared, and she went on to win the Telstra Business Woman of the Year Award.

After she told her compelling story, as she walked off stage, I ran up to her and said, "I am your 40-year-old self. I'm not in the darkroom yet, but I would love to know what advice you would give me." To my surprise, she took both of my hands, looked me square in the eye, and said words I will never forget. "Do you have someone in your life?" Shocked, I told her yes, but that I was keeping him a secret for now from the kids. "Do you love him?" She asked. "Of course, absolutely with all my heart," I stated. She then said, "I thought that by living with my parents, my children would see what real love was and that by working hard and being successful, I would show them a successful life. Years later, they told me that none of that ever mattered to them and that all they only ever wanted was to see me happy and for ME to SHOW them what REAL LOVE was. So go and introduce him to your girls; it's time."

Many years later, one of my daughters took my hand the other day and said, "Mum, I'm so glad you moved on. I never knew what real love was until I saw the way he looked at you and you at him. He treats you like a princess and your voice always changes to a soft musical happy tone when you see or talk to him. I now know what real love is and I will never accept anything less." This made me freeze. These words were the same that the lady on the beach had told me all those years before, as well as the wise words of Julie Adams from Chemo@Home.

Kian changed my life. Through his supportive life-changing encouragement and massive belief in me, I decided to take a major risk in my life. After 22 years, I would leave the corporate world to follow my dream of being a teacher and a full-time artist. I am currently in the second year of my degree and am a full-time artist, teaching kids and adults art. This is the best thing I ever did—the thing I was born to do. But then, one day, I thought, who would hire a middle-aged teacher heading towards her 50s? I then decided I needed to stand out. I wished to become a well-known, famous and successful Australian artist.

One day I attended a networking event and noticed a live artist painting. A few hours later, they auctioned it off, raising $4000 for charity. I asked who the event organizer was and introduced myself to yet another person who would change my life forever, Pat Luca. I insisted that he involve me in his next event and I also said, rather confidently, that my painting would raise a lot more than $4000. (I didn't tell him that I hadn't painted a thing for ten years, but I felt that wasn't at the time necessary to mention.)

Almost a year later, I was surprised to get a call from Pat Luca. A man of his word was calling me asking if I could paint at an event on Rottnest Island. Around 500 people would be attending on fancy million-dollar boats where all of the who's who of Perth would be there to raise money for Telethon. He mentioned that Shakey Jakey had pulled out at the last minute and that wasn't I the artist who said I could paint? I said, "Yes, of course, I would do it! When is it?" He replied very quickly that it was in five days. Of course, I replied yes rather too confidently and then I hung up and decided to turn my panic into passion. I quickly discovered an amazing New York artist called Iris Scott. She painted using only her hands and fingers. How hard could that be, right? So there I was, five days later, painting a giant mermaid live using only my hands, and before I knew it, the auctioneer had reached $26,000. He said, "Hey Jo, would you do two paintings?" I quickly replied, "yes," and suddenly, I had raised $52,000 for Telethon, MND and MSWA. (Was it still too late to mention that I hadn't painted a thing in over ten years until that very day?)

After that, I became trendy and went on to paint not just landscapes and abstracts but also realistic portraits of celebrities and politicians. They all personally signed my artwork, such as Scott Morrison, the then Prime Minister of Australia, Mark McGowan, the premier of WA, Daniel Ricciardo, Ray Meager (Alf from Home and Away), Nat Fyfe, Nic Naitanui, Damian Martin, Bryce Cotton, Kelly Slater and Anthony Mundine. (I profusely thank Pat Luca for organizing the majority of these.)

I have raised over $187,000 for charities such as MND, Telethon, Zero2Hero Youth Suicide, MSWA, Dr. Charlie Teo Foundation, Charlies Hope, Millstar Foundation, Breast Cancer Awareness, Men's Depression, Heart Foundation and Leukemia Foundation, as well as many others including personally helping terminally ill children and their families. (I'm hoping to reach my personal goal of $200,000 before the end of this year, 2022.)

I then came across another life-changing opportunity that suddenly presented itself. The chance to have my own gallery in the very well-to-do area in Perth. A street called Bayview Terrace Claremont. This exciting opportunity caused me to think about asking an international fashion designer if he would like to share my shop with me and create wearable art - where fashion meets art. Applying for grants and gaining sponsors, we ran events of fashion shows and art. I made motivational art classes that involved local businesses and combined art with food, wine, community, culture with opera music, and orchestras with harp and jazz singers. These events were massive hits and brought joy and inspiration to people who needed uplifting during Covid.

A fantastic friend of mine, Ron Wise, allowed me to collaborate with him to create an Australian Marine "Collagin." A gin infused with marine collagen with an Australian Barrier Reef Fish painting where I designed the label to make the fish appear to be swimming inside the gin. My artwork was also transferred onto a gown made from the fibers of an acacia tree using vibrant eucalyptus inks, which were a one-of-a-kind wearable art sustainable design.

I appeared on two Foxtel talkshows called Hello Darling hosted by Barbara McNaught and The Couch hosted by Fred Mafrica, where I painted them as they interviewed me live on the show, and I discussed my charity work. Sometimes I would paint using only a rose as a paintbrush or my hands. Barbara interviewed me about my life and how I have transformed to help others through my art. She also allowed me to speak as her guest at the Crown Towers for International Women's Day (just like Julie Adams all those years before, but this time it was my turn to tell my story.)

I began my speech (and ended it with,) "If I can help just one woman in this room, then my journey has been worth it." As I left the stage, a woman shyly approached me, took my hands, and said, "I'm that woman. I had no idea I was coming today, but my mum surprised me and brought me to hear you speak. I want you to know that I now know what I need to do." This lady had no idea how happy she made me feel. However, after she left, I had a line of women wanting to tell me that they were also 'that woman.'

Two years later, I still receive messages from women who heard me speak that day to say that 'they are that woman.' The women I have helped change the direction of their life for the better. This has inspired me to continue telling my story to help guide and uplift women (or men) to know they can move forward.

Another exciting event was when I painted a giant tiger using the signed boxing gloves of Anthony Mundine to the song of "eye of the tiger." At the song's end, the lighting went to darkness so that you could see the glow in the dark paint revealing the tiger's eyes. This painting and gloves were also auctioned off on the night for charity.

My story is to tell people that your only limit is your imagination. Those who think magic doesn't exist will never find it. But it's there and it has always been inside of every one of us. The trick is we all need to uplift and empower each other. We need to find our passion and trust the journey, no matter how scary it seems. I could never have been on this fantastic journey without the love and support of my family and less than a handful of amazing friends. Once I let go of people who brought me down or created negativity, life replaced them with amazing and encouraging people. I am about to hold my first art exhibition overseas and open another gallery this year. Without jumping in with both feet and trusting the manifestation process, this would have never happened.

I have recently been chosen to be in a documentary called "Project Manifest." Ten of us have been chosen to document our journeys over ten months. One thing I know about manifesting is that you need to trust the process completely. When you believe in what you want to come about, you have to expect that things you may consider obstacles will come your way. The trick is to keep and maintain your focus and those obstacles have appeared to direct you to the right place, the right person, and the direction that you will need to change for your manifestation to come about. If you lose focus and instead focus entirely on the obstacles and say, "Why me? This isn't what I asked for!" The universe will continue to give you even more, blocks because that is what you are focusing on! Trust the process, ride the waves. You will lose people and gain people along the way but know that you will get where you need to go, even if it's not quite how you imagined getting there.

I am now ready to receive and begin a new journey of abundance and watch my art career grow! I start my day every day by chanting thank you, thank you, you three times before my feet touch the ground. Appreciation and gratefulness is the absolute key to starting every day. Not a day slips by without my feet touching the beach sand or in nature, where I affirm three times that I am what I am. This knowledge has expanded my journey of abundance. It has taught me just to be and to trust the journey deeply.

One thing's for sure, I wouldn't change what happened in my life, or I wouldn't have had my two beautiful girls or met my wonderful husband, Kian. But I also feel that sometimes just like climbing a mountain, it's a long, painful struggle to get there and you take many risks and want to give up many times along the way. But if you can just put your fears aside and focus on your goal, you will reach the summit and appreciate it even more. I am so grateful for where my journey has taken me; now, I want to give back and help others on similar trips. There is a way out.

You can move past your wounds and transform then into wisdom; Just like Dorothy from the Wizard of Oz, you have the power within yourself. I never thought I would find love again, but I married the most wonderful man who every day makes me and my girls feel so loved, valued and believed in. I finally know what real love is. I hope I have inspired even just one woman or man to alchemize their wounds into wisdom. Just have faith and believe. The rest will come. Now that I have gained wings, I can soar and finally do anything I set my mind to do.

"As soon as healing takes place, go out and heal somebody else."

~Maya Angelou

CHAPTER SIX

—◦◦◦◦—

Transforming Generational Curses into Generational Blessings

By Catherine Schwark

"A child must pay for the sins of their parents."

Exodus 20:5

It was a different era back in the 1960s and '70s in America. The Western Industrialized World was in turmoil with civil rights, anti-Vietnam War protests, and the Woman's Liberation Movement, all demonstrating to effect great political, intellectual, and cultural change against the patriarchal political and societal rule. People of color began demanding their equal rights; students were being killed on their college campus by our military for daring to protest, and women were burning their bras. It was the decade that also began transforming the patriarchal nuclear family.

My father wasn't like the oppressors of the time. He tried to do right by Mom and married her when they learned she was pregnant (Mom was 17, Dad 19). But there was one problem. Mom was Roman Catholic, and Dad was Lutheran. The Church would NEVER accept my Lutheran father, who refused to convert his religion to Catholicism. And then there was this sex out of wedlock situation. That would be two mortal sins going into the marriage. My aunt had recently entered the convent to become a nun, and Grandma was a regular tither, so The Church agreed to marry my parents on the condition that all offspring be raised in the one true faith, Roman Catholic. Naturally, there would be plenty of offspring since, according to The Church, any form of artificial contraception or birth control is considered intrinsically evil, and well, my parents were still adolescents themselves....

So, they were married in a small, private ceremony at The Church, Mom in a purple dress....

They had seven children in the next thirteen years. I was number four, smack dab in the middle. I wasn't a wanted baby; truth be told, none of us were. Mom was 21 years old and already had the diapers, feeding and training of three toddlers to deal with. By the time I came along, there was no time to hold, feed, or nurture yet another baby. Bottles would be prompted on pillows placed alongside my infant body. From a side-angle, my newborn lips would attempt to suckle droplets of milk as drops streamed down my cheeks and into my ears. I gasped a belly full of air for each droplet of milk I swallowed, but there was no time for burping.

We weren't a *Leave It to Beaver* or *Father Knows Best* family, but our basic needs were met. We were creative and played outside all day with all that nature has to offer. We were happy kids without a care in the world. I never heard arguing or a raised voice in the home. All was good, until it wasn't....

It was a normal sunny afternoon, and I was helping my dad carry the reck room furniture up the basement stairs and out to the rented truck. Dad is especially quiet today; in fact, he's not saying a word. I understand that we were moving our basement furniture to a new place and I could hardly *believe* it! We must have come into some money! I mean, we're doing better than the other neighborhood families if we can afford to have TWO homes! Well, the other is only an apartment, and I have no clue why we need an apartment, but one thing is for certain, and that is, WE MUST BE R-I-C-H, RICH if we can afford this!

I found myself staring into the distance at the window sill, like a dog waiting for its owner, anxiously awaiting Dad's return from our new place. But he never came. I lost the first piece of my heart the day I accepted he wasn't ever coming home. I learned from the talk of the neighborhood kids – my parents were divorced. Turns out my parents weren't any better at communicating with their children than they were with each other. Divorced? What does that even mean?! (It was the early '70s, and no one was divorced.) All the neighborhood kids knew about it was that it meant that my dad didn't live with us anymore.

Turns out divorce is also a grave mortal sin in the Roman Catholic Church. My traditional church went old school and pulled scripture from the Old Testament to ensure that they *"Prepare a place to slaughter his children for the sins of their ancestors"* Isaiah 14:21. In other words, me. I was the one selected to be slaughtered for the sins of my parents.

"Who defines us before we define ourselves?"

Jeff Brown

On this special, sacred day, consecrated company joined us for the ceremony. My neck cranked over my shoulder as I watched from my designated seat—front pew, last seat furthest from the aisle –as the bishop paraded slowly down the aisle, which was white carpeted just for today's sacred sacrament.

Yes, he certainly was different from the Black Robes I saw every week. His garment was a long white vestment adorned with ribbons of gold trim. An enormous solid gold pectoral cross hung from his neck, and his hand was adorned with a large ruby ring, a symbol of his commitment and marriage to Christ and The Church. The miter headdress that sat upon his head was higher than an alien's cone head.

Symbolizing his high rank within the Church, he carried his crosier gold staff high above his head, nearly equal to the stained-glass windows lining the walls of the brick building. We were supposed to feel blessed that he graced us with his presence; this was a *very special day.* He walked up the two stairs that led to the altar, then slowly turned to face the congregation from the pulpit. His towering and imposing presence appeared larger than life.

In the front pew to the left of the altar sat all the little eight and nine-year-old boys dressed in dark suits and polished shoes, with their hair greased down into place. The girls fidgeted in their spots in the front pew to the right of the altar, with their faces all aglow. Their long wavy curls bounced under their elegant veils. Each wore pure snow-white dresses with matching white hand gloves.

Well, that is – all of the girls except for *me.* I wore a yellow dress, yellow to show my church community that I was a stained little girl, signaling that I was less worthy to be in the presence of such goodness and purity. My fine, stringy hair was like cooked noodles springing from my scalp.

One by one, the bishop asked each child a biblical question to see if they were worthy of this holiest of holy occasions in a Roman Catholic's life – the Sacrament of the Holy Eucharist, the bread and wine, the body and blood of Jesus Christ. He began his questioning with the boy furthest from the aisle on the left side and was going to end with me, the little girl in the yellow dress in the last seat furthest from the aisle on the right.

I didn't hear any of the questions he asked the boys. The thoughts in my head were busy and loud: *Where is everyone? Why is grandma the only one here I know? What's wrong with me? Why am I not good enough? Why did I have to wear a yellow dress? Every other girl here is dressed in white. My two older sisters wore white dresses for their First Communion. What's wrong with me?*

What have I done? Why am I bad? Why is no one here to celebrate me? Why is my First Communion a dirty little secret?

I was jolted back to the parish when the questioning began on the girl's side of the aisle. My nine-year-old body sat there with knees knocking and teeth grinding. My eyes stayed glued to the floor, as my yellow dress in the sea of whiteness was proof enough that I wasn't worthy of being there. I attuned my ears to each question he asked. He began with the aisle child; nope, I didn't know the answer to that one. Then he moved to the next girl in the pew; nope, I didn't know the answer to that one either.

It took everything I had in me to stop myself from bawling and sobbing right then and there. He was going to ask me a question that I wouldn't know the answer to and prove once and for all to the entire church community that I was bad, stained, unworthy and deserved to be in that yellow dress. *Please, God, please,* my soul cried out. I couldn't take any more humiliation.

When it was my turn, he waited until I slowly lifted my head and forced myself to look at him.

His thunderous voice bellowed, "What do you say at the end of a prayer?"

What?! Is this a trick question? I know the answer to this one – everyone knows the answer to this one. It's amen, right?! I'm certain that's the correct answer. I hope this isn't a trick question.

My meek voice sputtered out, "Amen."

Whew. No choir of angels broke out in song of praises, but I did answer correctly. Thank you, God!

After the ceremony, my grandmother and I walked the seven blocks back to her house in silence. I wanted to ask, *where was everyone? Why did no one come today? Why is there no party for me afterward? Why don't I get a cake to celebrate and religious gifts such as a cross necklace or cards with cash like my sisters did? Why is no one taking pictures of me on my special day?* But we didn't speak of such things in our family. Silence was golden. You were considered "good" if you remained silent. I knew it was because of the yellow dress. It was a symbol for all to see how stained, dirty, bad, and unworthy I really was. *Why did I have to wear the yellow dress? What did I do? Why am I bad?* These thoughts raced over and over again in my mind. Even on the walk home, I kept my eyes peeled to the ground. At nine years old, I didn't know I was being punished for my parents' "sins."

By forcing me to wear a yellow dress on the day of my First Communion, The Church may just as well have taken an electric cattle branding iron and burnt the numbers 666 upon my forehead for all eternity because the unworthiness and shame I wore from that day on was more obvious than a Hell's Angel's tattooed body. Unfortunately, the shame bestowed upon me that day was truly the gateway for numerous terrifying, traumatic incidents to occur in the future.

"If you can't change it, change your attitude."

Iniquity means that we are bent or pulled toward a particular sin. A generational iniquity is behind the sin that has been practiced in a previous generation. A brief synopsis of what happened after the divorce is that my mother went from a mom to a drunken barfly who exposed me to numerous pedophiles. My dad went from a father to a hardcore alcoholic who never left his apartment unless it was to work or buy more cigarettes and beer. The pedophiles I was exposed to could already tell from the 666 shame-stained stamp upon my face that I was an easy target for their perverted pleasures. As assured by The Church's curse, I followed in my parents' footsteps and, for decades, abused alcohol to numb my pain.

Even though I stared at a life-sized, attention-grabbing sculpture of Christ's crucified body hanging on the cross that stood behind the altar every Sunday, for the life of me, I couldn't see, feel, or come to know Jesus anywhere in that church. Yet, somewhere deep inside my childhood heart, I knew that this shame was being inflicted by man, not God.

While in the depths of my dark abyss, it was challenging to find my way. I was grasping, searching, and reaching for any ray of light, even a flicker of a flame, that would show me the way. My hands were callused for my efforts; my body contoured like a pretzel; the blood in my veins pulsated and throbbed; my brain blocked, and my spirit sparsely safe.

There is a slew of traumatic stories, each with lessons of their own, from the time of the yellow dress incident that I could share but let's get to the good part…the part where I eventually managed to scrape up those scattered stained shards of my soul and glue them together to form a new picture, a new story, much like the pieces in the stained-glass windows hanging in St. Augustine's Catholic Church.

When I finally met God is when my life was completely out of control. I tried many times to quit drinking on my own. I made many unkept promises to others that I would, yet I couldn't. I had gotten pulled over for drinking and driving, and still, I continued to drink and drive. One day I found myself curled up in the fetal position on the floor sobbing. I was so desperate, anguished and hopeless. In an agony that would equal Mary watching her son being crucified on the cross I cried out loud to God, "Please help me!"

Now in my messed up religious and alcoholic mind, I thought the all-powerful God would just wave his magic wand over me, and the desire to drink would be removed, but that's not how it worked. I continued to drink. I continued to drink *and* drive. I continued to drink and drive and got pulled over. I hadn't even been to court on the previous offence, and I got pulled over *again*. I say that second DWI was God's answer to my prayer because I quickly got my butt to treatment after that. After my 30-day inpatient education, I entered the rooms of 12-Steppers.

I sat in a dingy room with long brown tables and cold metal chairs. People from all walks of life sat at the table with me. Each shared their own unique story of how their lives had become unmanageable and what they did to overcome their drinking issues. Laughter and joy reigned. Society had labels for these folks, too – it mattered not if they were medical doctors or felons – society labeled them as the downtrodden, the sinners, the drunkards, and the losers.

But do you want to know what I found in those dingy rooms? I found love, faith, brotherly kindness, charity, humility, diligence, and temperance. I found all the attributes of Christ in the dark, dingy rooms with long tables and cold metal chairs. I found the Jesus I had searched for in the church community in the downtrodden, the sinners, the drunkards, and the losers. Someone said, "Don't let the Christians keep you from Christ," and they were right.

Little did I know that God's mysterious and mystical magic was in my mess. The irony is that God used the façade of the goodness of The Church to show me all that is ugly in the world that left me cursed and in darkness and then used the downtrodden, the sinners, the drunkards, and the losers to show me all that is beautiful and good in the world and my way back to wholeness is not lost on me. They taught me about spirituality. All addiction programs have a Higher Power, and they show you how to discover/create/ find a God that loves *you*. I began having my own sacred mystical experiences.

But there was still work to do. The 12-Steppers taught me what I needed to know to quit drinking, but those traumas ingrained in childhood aren't so easily removed. The reason I began to drink in the first place was still there, waiting to eat me alive. It's the wounds that no one sees that are the most painful. Suppressed emotions for survival necessity usually leads one to disassociate from self, and I had most certainly disassociated from myself. Once I set the alcohol down, I still needed to bring to light what my invisible enemy was. Not knowing what the invisible enemy is, is like swinging in the dark. The darkness (unconscious) is not the opposite of light (consciousness); it is the absence of it. Awareness is key, and you can't change it if you can't see it. It was no longer about understanding but *inner*standing.

"Be transformed by the renewal of your mind."

Romans 12:2

I began to comprehend that I needed to reprogram my subconscious mind. I began to see, know and believe that I didn't have to accept The Church's curse. That I was an innocent little girl left vulnerable to be fed to the wolves by a "curse" that man inflicted upon me, not God. The scripture *"be transformed by the renewal of your m*ind" Romans 12:2 became my mantra. I saw that I wasn't born with my negative self-image and self-worth. I was programmed this way. And while this wasn't my fault, it was my responsibility to change it, to reprogram it, to activate it. No Prince Charming's kiss was going to save me or turn me snow white. I learned that I didn't need to be saved or rescued, I needed knowledge of my own power and how to access it. If it was to be, it was up to me. Albert Einstein said, "We cannot solve our problems with the same thinking that we used when we created them." The 12 Steppers taught me that my "stinking thinking" or negative thought patterns could increase daily life stressors, promote anxiety, increase depression, or even trigger a relapse. I learned from a mentor that by saying, *"now I am the voice,"* I am telling my subconscious that I am in control now. I hold the power to shift my mindset and take control of my subconscious behaviors at any moment. This power to question myself, my thoughts and my focus is my magic wand to creating my world. I am my own liberator from the jailers of my mind.

I began to realize that I was the one I'd been waiting for. I am the ancestor that changes everything in my bloodline. I am the golden light in human form brought to earth with a higher purpose. I am the one that will change my great-great-grandchildren's legacy. I was chosen to *mold the clay into something new.* It's time for the generational curses to be transformed into generational blessings!

I've made it my life's mission and purpose to leave an impactful, inspiring, and illuminating family and community legacy that impresses a positive influence on Seven Generations into the future regarding health, wealth, love, and connection. I will transform the generational curse bestowed upon an innocent little girl in a yellow dress to leaving futuristic generational birthright blessings of snow white, self-confident SUPERSTARS. (Who remembers the old SNL skit with Mary Katherine Gallagher auditioning for the talent show at Monica's Catholic School in her little plaid skirt, white pressed blouse, and monogrammed vest? After her obnoxious audition where she falls into a rack of metal chairs, she jumps right back up, throws her arms up in a victorious V, and says, "*SUPERSTAR!*")

The New Covenant (or the New Testament) is the promise that God made to humanity that forgives sin and restores fellowship with those whose hearts are turned toward him. Jesus Christ is the mediator of the New Covenant, and his death on the cross is the basis of the promise. The Old Covenant is written in stone (such as the children must pay for their parents' sins), but the New Covenant is written in our hearts.

I will give you a new heart and put a new spirit in you; I will remove from you your heart of stone and give you a heart of flesh.

And I will put my Spirit in you and move you to follow my decrees and be careful to keep my laws."
~ Ezekiel 36:26-27

I am often reminded to love the unlovable, the voices that have been silenced. Remember that our own inner child is a future ancestor and that love is the answer. Love is always the answer. And when you struggle to find any resemblance of love in this world, call upon your Higher Power, Jesus, or the Holy Spirit. And then be ready for the work to begin.

READER'S REFLECTION: Think of a time when you've had a "yellow dress" incident. Who have you handed authority of your destiny over to? How did your incident impact the beliefs you've held about yourself? What will you do to turn your curse into a blessing?

"**Wounds will turn into wisdom, when they are washed with forgiveness, bound up with precious lessons learned, and strengthen with the courage to make life better.**"

~ Paul Wong

CHAPTER SEVEN

---∞⟨∿⟩∞---

Inner Work to Outer Peace
By Nadia Elmagrabi

*"No tree, it is said, can grow to heaven unless
its roots reach down to hell."*

– C.G. Jung

O n the morning of May 15, 2020, my husband asked me if I'd like to look at a house in Northern Michigan. During a call with our son's teachers the night before, we both realized that the chances of our kids returning to their beloved private school in the fall were anything but certain. If they did go back, most likely, it would be a very different experience than what we wanted for them. This was the nail in the coffin, so to speak, for us continuing to live in the Detroit area. I loved the life we created for ourselves. We had great friends, community, grandparents nearby, and all the conveniences I depended on — yoga studios, great restaurants, and activities for the kids.

I spent the last two months clearing out and organizing our entire house from top to bottom and, in the process, created my dream office. I was excited to start seeing clients face to face again and to have a place to meet with them.

When Adam asked me to look at a house four hours away, I was surprised. We were confined to our home for the past two months. So, the idea of taking a road trip was appealing. What did we have to lose? He showed the kids and me the pictures of the house he wanted to see.

The house we were going to look at was in a Country Club on a golf course. Unlike Adam, I had no desire to live on a golf course. But as we pulled into the community, all I saw were trees. It was a golf course surrounded by miles and miles of woods. I couldn't believe my eyes when I saw a trailhead about 100 yards from the driveway as we pulled up. Ever since living in Telluride, I have yearned to be able to walk out my front door and be in nature. I deeply desired it. Our family amongst the trees were the pictures I had around my house and saved on my phone. Our daily walks in our Detroit suburb neighborhood were lovely, but nothing compared to being in the woods. We all loved the house. It just felt right. It was spacious and comfortable, with huge windows overlooking a pond. It felt nourishing to my soul.

As we were driving home, it felt surreal. Daily life sure would be different there. I loved my life. I didn't want to leave the place where there was so much supporting us. But life was different now. We had gone without so much of those for the past two months. My husband hadn't been to his office; I was meeting clients on Zoom; our two boys were at home. Our dependency on the life we once had was gone—what a strange place to be.

We built our current house ten years prior, and we loved it. It was the only home my boys knew. Despite all my reservations, something deep within me said this was the right thing to do. "Strike while the iron is hot" is the phrase that kept going through my mind. I was not one to make spur-of-the-moment decisions, but I knew that if we wanted to make a move like this-the opportunity was now. It truly felt like divine orchestration.

So, we did it, and it happened fast! It took less than two weeks from the moment we had the idea to look at the house to buy it and sell ours. And just like that, we were moving!

Some of our friends and family thought we were nuts. They couldn't understand why we would leave our life where we "had everything" and move somewhere so remote. The truth is, we felt stifled by our life and the community where we were living. There was increasing pressure to think and believe in a certain way, which was NOT in alignment with what was true for us. So, it was becoming increasingly apparent that we needed a significant change.

That was over two years ago, and I could not be happier with our decision to move to the woods. I'm so glad I followed my intuition and stepped into the unknown. There was no way to know if it would work out, but I trusted my husband and his intuition, and together we leaped. Now, we both work from home, and instead of being ships that pass in the night like in our old life, we have ample time together. We both have space in our house where we can work uninterrupted and then come together when we choose. Our children enjoy golf, sailing, baseball, and skiing. Of course, there have been challenges, especially for my older son and leaving his friends. But overall, we all feel it was the right move.

TIMING IS EVERYTHING

Had this opportunity come to us earlier, it's doubtful I would have been open to it. Adam and I were in such a different place in our marriage. In 2019, we were on the verge of splitting up if something didn't change.

In May 2019, I trained outside Philadelphia with Carol Bowman to learn how to do Past Life Regressions. It was something that I deeply desired to do. I had read her book *Children's Past Lives* six months previous and was thrilled when I discovered that she trained therapists to do regression work. Ever since my college years in the 90s, I have been intrigued with the concept of reincarnation and past lives. I knew that this was the next step for me in my work with clients.

Even though I had read a lot about past lives, I had never experienced a regression. Over the years, I have connected with several psychics and channelers who have told me about different past lives that were relevant to me in my current life. I deeply recognized these experiences, which helped me with my inner work and soul growth. I longed to know how to connect to these memories on my own.

I had my first regression during the training. The woman I partnered with had done Carol's training before, and was adept at holding space and doing regression work. I would like to offer a trigger warning here before I go into the regression details because it includes violence and sexual assault. Please don't go any further if it will be upsetting to your nervous system to read such things.

My partner took me into a relaxation process after we discussed my core concern which had to do with a fear of being seen fully. After the relaxation, she had me repeat the phrase we came up with, "I'm not safe." I repeated it a few times, and she asked me what I was experiencing. Immediately, I sensed that someone was pushing my face into a dirt floor, and I was being kicked. Then, as the images became more apparent, I realized my husband and children were assaulting me. My guide asked me to go back to just before this experience to understand how this came to be.

I saw myself with a band of nomads. It felt like the 1800s in Egypt, and I lived in a little village along the Nile. The nomadic group I was with was my original people, and I left them years before to marry this husband. He mistreated me, as did the rest of the people from this village. I had very dark skin and was lean. These villagers looked down upon my people, as did my husband. He frequently beat and sexually assaulted me. We had three boys together. When I discovered my people were coming through the village, I saw this as my opportunity to escape a difficult life. Before I found the nomadic group, I shared my plan with a woman in the town.

I experienced such peace and relief when I found my people. They welcomed me with open arms. It felt so natural and comforting to be with them. I was sitting with the women, and we were braiding each other's hair. It didn't last long, though, as the village woman told my husband before we could leave. So, he came to find me and drag me, kicking and screaming through the streets to our dirt-floor house. He beat me, and my children joined in as they were also so angry that I was going to leave them. I never fully recovered from the injuries I sustained from that beating. I harbored resentment and anger toward my husband for making my life difficult.

My husband died in that life. My eldest sons had moved out of the village, but my youngest son stayed. After my husband died, I devoted myself to prayer and the spiritual practice I grew up doing. I lived a tranquil and calm life and kept to myself. My youngest son lived nearby with his family and cared for me into my old age.

My expert guide helped me go through the process of doing what I needed to integrate and put what I needed from that life to rest. I forgave my husband and saw him from the soul perspective that he didn't know any better. She asked if I recognized any of the people in that life in my current life, and I did! My husband in that life was my paternal grandfather, and my children were my dad in this life and my two sons. I felt such a strong recognition. I had the sense that I was my great, great, great, great grandmother in that life.

This experience helped me put so much into perspective in my current life. I feel the eternal connections with my sons and father and see that our relationships are much more than this lifetime. In a sense, the regression itself was the easy part. Even though it was violent and unpleasant, I was somewhat removed from the experience. I felt strong emotions, but I was still very aware that it was a memory and not happening in real-time. It's as if part of me was in that timeline, and part of me was in my current timeline.

The most challenging part of the experience for me was coming home to my husband. He was not the same husband in that lifetime, but we had our difficulties in THIS lifetime. We were like ships passing in the night. He worked all day Monday through Friday, and I often worked on the weekends and evenings. I had recently started a business with a friend where we were selling crystals and doing crystal healing sessions for groups of people.

I loved the idea and the concept, but I was not enjoying the lifestyle. It took me away from my family and required spending a lot of money to get it off the ground. We didn't have a solid business plan, and it was asking more of me than I wanted to give. My husband felt the strain of me being gone, and I felt the pressure of depleting my bank account to start this business. I was beginning to realize that it was more of a fantasy than a viable business.

When I left for the regression training, I felt angry and hurt that my husband was not supportive of my business endeavors, and he was feeling neglected and abandoned by me. When I returned, that anger continued to fester until we had a blow-up. I told him about the regression and the feelings of anger that I experienced during that lifetime. He recognized that I was still holding that anger but directing it toward him! This was a pivotal moment because there was truth to his reflection. It was there and then that we decided to get couples counseling.

Up until that point, I had dedicated my life to doing self-work. Early in our marriage, I was in psychoanalysis for six and a half years, where I went to therapy and free-associated four or five times a week. During that process, I explored every nook and cranny of my subconscious mind, or so I thought. We can only go so far in any type of self-work.

When circumstances change, new lessons and aspects of growth appear to work through. During my psychoanalysis, I dug deep and cleared a lot of what troubled me from childhood and adolescence.

I became more self-confident and released the anxiety and ruminating thoughts plaguing me. I worked through my anger and resentments in the beginning phases of my relationship with my husband. But this anger ran deep, and my relationship with my husband triggered it.

It was easy for me to blame Adam and direct my anger toward him. Don't get me wrong; we had a great relationship most of the time. We enjoyed each other's company and worked well together navigating life and parenthood. However, there were times when I felt he wasn't supporting me. I was looking for validation from Adam and wanted him to be my cheerleader and encourage me with my endeavors. He was the ultimate truth teller and couldn't and wouldn't give me something that he didn't feel was genuine.

In these times, I felt like we were battling each other head-to-head. I felt like he was going against me and not supporting me. This situation with the business was one of those instances. It created a divide in our relationship, and I felt alone. Through therapy with one of my amazing mentors, I could unpack my anger and see that I was projecting the anger I had at ALL men onto my husband.

I learned during my regression that I had spent a lifetime unsupported and undermined for years. I was carrying this wound with me into this life. I realized my husband was supporting me and always had been. He was also there for our family. I was the one who had gone astray. I was the one who was trying to make something work that was shiny and pretty on the outside but was ultimately taking me away from my family and the life I cherished.

During one of our sessions, our therapist asked on a scale of one to ten how committed we were to making the relationship work. When I said ten, I could visibly see and feel my husband relax and soften. He thought I was more committed to my projects than to him and our family. I finally realized how pursuing this business was not serving my family or me.

The truth is, while the idea was appealing, the day in and day out of it was not fulfilling and left me feeling depleted and unsatisfied. Until then, I worked with clients individually as a massage therapist, psychotherapist, or health coach. I naturally go deep with people and hold space for them as they unearth and process what they need to work through. Adding past life regressions to my repertoire was what my heart was calling for; my clients needed me to help them get past their unconscious blocks.

After the training, I began doing regressions for people. Immediately, I felt nourished by the work and realized I wanted to return primarily to my one-on-one practice, separate from the crystal business. I told my husband my plan, and he was again relieved and now very supportive. It was an intricate and challenging process to separate from my business partner and the business.

Step by step, I did what it took to get myself out. My business partner had a different experience with what we were doing, and she didn't want it to end. So, there were a lot of difficult conversations. I had the support from my husband, therapist, and friends during this process. It took about nine months and serendipitously was complete just before the world went into lockdown.

Once it was over, I felt so free and relaxed, and I cherished the time I had at home with my family over those following months. There were struggles with school, my work with clients, and not seeing friends and family, but my husband and I became closer and more connected than ever. I no longer had that underlying feeling of anger toward him. I no longer saw him as being against me. Everything about our relationship and the way we interacted softened. We became much more in tune with one another. We enjoyed being together as a family.

Without the relationship with my husband, I would never have had the opportunity to learn valuable lessons. We met in our early thirties and had a lot of life experiences to bring to the marriage.

We both were set in our ways to an extent. Until I met him, I had never been in a relationship with someone I could imagine marrying. Months before we met, I came to terms with the possibility that I may not find someone to settle down with and have children. I had also said no to two romantic relationships that were not serving my needs in the past six months. I had finally learned the lesson that I'd rather be alone than with someone just to be in a relationship.

When I walked into a frame shop to pick up some prints I had ordered for my office, I was not expecting to meet my future husband. He was standing at a poster bin with a print I had been looking at when I placed my initial order. I went directly to the container in the back of the shop, worried that he would buy it before me. I asked if he was planning to buy my poster. I didn't even notice him, although apparently, he had his eye on me the entire time. We got to talking, and by the time I left, I accepted his offer of a date for the next day! Three months later, he bought me that print which is now hanging above our fireplace.

I had moved back to the Detroit area, where I grew up, about two years before we met to go back to school for Clinical & Humanistic Psychology at the Center for Humanistic Studies in Detroit. I had been away from Detroit for about twelve years when I went to college, moved to Colorado, went to school for Massage Therapy, worked at resort spas, and traveled around the world. After taking a course combining embodiment practices, meditation, psychology, and massage therapy in Kauai, I planned to complete my master's program in psychology and then continue my travels. However, the Universe had other plans for me.

About three weeks and several dates after meeting at the frame shop, I was giving a massage late one night and had a mystical experience. I would take my massage table to client's' houses after the workday at the mental health clinic. I was at a house with huge windows overlooking a lake on this particular night. The lighting was dim, and the moonlight was shimmering on the water. There was relaxing music playing, and the smell of lavender permeated the air.

Spontaneously, I left that scene and found myself in front of a large screen with a kind, wise woman speaking to me. On my right were three tiers of souls. Everyone, including myself, was a luminescent being. The female elder gestured toward the rows of souls and said, "This is who you're going to marry." I looked over and immediately recognized the man I had met just three weeks before. That was it. I was back giving the massage again. It was an extremely vivid experience, and I had no consciousness of my physical body when it happened. I was entirely in that scene. The message I received from that experience was to let my guard down and allow myself be vulnerable.

I had been so jaded by love in the past, and I didn't trust men. I didn't trust them to do what they said they would do, and I certainly didn't trust them with my heart. I had a history of choosing men who didn't give me the attention I wanted. During my master's program, I began therapy for the first time. I started putting together pieces of my history of choosing the "wrong" kind of guy. I realized that the attention I wanted was from my father, and I was using these relationships to try to fill this need, yet they were all incapable.

My family immigrated to the United States from England when I was three. My father was a physician from Egypt and met my mother during one of his rotations in Cardiff. They were married nine months later, and then moved my brother and me to the U.S. four years afterwards. My parents were dedicated to making a good life for our family.

Together we explored what this new land had to offer. We frequently traveled overseas to see family. It was the four of us at home, and even though my physical needs were met, I longed for more. We didn't talk about emotions and what we wanted out of life. We enjoyed funny movies, good food, being together, and being with friends. But I often felt like I wasn't good enough, and I craved attention and being noticed for my gifts from those I loved.

My father worked hard and left the child-raising to my mother. My mom was the ultimate homemaker and wanted the best for us, but she didn't know how to connect with me on an emotional level. My dad mostly seemed bothered by my existence. He was an excellent provider and supported whatever I wanted to do, but he was not interested in knowing who I was. I craved his attention, and as soon as I became a teenager, I started seeking that attention from the boys at school.

I experienced my first love at the age of fifteen. He was two years older and gave me all the attention I desired. He would pick me up in his vintage convertible Cadillac. We'd go out with friends or to the school hangouts. I loved being with him but didn't know how to share that. I had difficulty expressing my feelings even though they ran so deep. I was devastated when he returned from camp in the summer and told me he had fallen in love with another girl.

A part of me closed off after that relationship, and I never let my guard down again until I met my husband. After that first relationship, I had many other boyfriends but didn't allow myself surrender to them for fear of losing myself and getting hurt. I continued to choose boys and men who were okay being with me physically and not emotionally. And to be honest, that's all I wanted too.

It wasn't until I met Adam that I truly allowed myself to be vulnerable. This time it was different. He was honest with me like no one had ever been before. He did what he said he was going to do. He always planned our next date before our current one was over. I wasn't left waiting and wondering where I stood. He was completely upfront and candid with me. It felt so refreshing, and I could relax in the relationship!

Two years after our destined meeting at the frame shop, he asked me to marry him in the same spot. It was an immediate "Yes!" from me. Over the years, we have grown so much together. Our journey with parenting has been a significant growth experience for both of us. Many of the choices we make as parents go against the cultural norms, and I am so grateful we have been on the same page regarding big decisions for our family. Ten years ago, we both learned Transcendental Meditation to help us become more mindful and give ourselves the much-needed self-care time necessary when raising children. We both value high-quality good food and nutrition for our family. And we have flexible schedules that leave ample time to be together and for ourselves.

Through my work doing past life therapy, I have learned that often what is gnawing at us, bothering us, or affecting us, can be just under the surface of our awareness. Once it becomes conscious, it can be integrated and released. Countless times, I have heard from my clients that they no longer experience the unrelenting anxiety that they thought was a part of them, or the pit in their stomach that was always there has disappeared. Miraculously, those symptoms disappear once the client can identify the root of their trouble. Frequently it is sourced from another life, from another time and place. I know this is true for me. I no longer feel the anger that seemed part of me. Yes, I get angry, but it's no longer this low-level feeling that permeates everything.

As someone devoted to doing the inner work to know myself, I know that it never is entirely over. There is always more. As I grow and expand, I dig deeper and uncover more. The two go hand in hand. I've experienced five regressions, and each one has helped me discover aspects of my past selves that have affected me in this lifetime. Whether the experiences are positive or negative, they have been essential in my soul's evolution. It's rarely pleasant work. It can be challenging and painful, but the rewards are immeasurable.

Over the years, I've learned to follow the nudges and the small inner voice whispering to me. I feel it in my body when it's right for me to do something. Even though it may not make sense, or it may even be the "wrong" decision, there is something that I need to learn or understand that is helping me in my soul's evolution. I know that the deeper I go with my work, the more I can hold space for others to do their inner work. I'm also acutely aware that when I'm willing to face what's uncomfortable, I benefit from this wisdom, and everyone around me benefits as well.

"The experience of life should mature you. It is your choice to transform a memory into a wound or wisdom."

~ Sadhguru

CHAPTER EIGHT

---∞‿∞---

Shaken to the Core

By Maria Loper

That morning seemed like any other ordinary morning, little did I know!

My daughter Shannon and I got up. We got ready, jumped in my old green car from the 90s, and drove into town as usual. We parked in one of the high-rise parking spots in the middle of the city.

I was heading into my office job on Hereford Street, and Shannon was going to her beauty school on Manchester Street. Once in the city, we decided to swing by a café in the Triangle Centre to have breakfast before we went our separate ways.

As usual, Shan and I chatted, joked around a bit, had our breakfast, and then contemplated the eventual walk to our different destinations. Although, when I look back now, I did say to Shan that I felt a bit queasy that morning, which wasn't usual for me.

We then made our descent down the escalator to the streets below. I began walking a block to my five-story office building on Hereford Street, where my office was on the third floor of the Westpac building. Shan had to walk three to four blocks to her beauty course on Manchester Street.

Back then, I worked for the Maori Women's Welfare League in Christchurch as a manager for a small program called "Whanau Toko It Ora." This program supported high-needs families in the community. It was a role I enjoyed immensely. I was also well supported by many of the lovely old Kuia (elders) who surrounded me in the community.

Once at the office, I began my usual routine of unpacking my bag, turning on my computer, and arranging my schedule for the day. That morning, I was working on writing my monthly report, and I needed to collate multiple types of information into reportable outcomes.

Then, suddenly, there was a knock on my office door. I wasn't expecting any visitors, so I wondered who it might be. It was my brother-in-law, Frank. He'd come to see me as he was working on a project and wanted to get my opinion on a few things and to know if I wanted to collaborate with him. Back then, Frank was working in the drug and alcohol sector in Christchurch. Well, he hadn't been talking to me for long when everything suddenly took a nasty turn for the worst!

The whole building began to rumble and shake violently, and the floor and the walls started to contort in unnatural positions that I knew were otherworldly. I felt like I was on an amusement ride from hell. To stay on my feet, I had to squat down low to the ground to keep my center of balance. I was also positioned behind my desk at the other end of the office, and I couldn't get close to the door. As what I was experiencing was so far outside of my usual grounded reality, I didn't know what to do. I froze like a deer in the headlights!

Since the situation didn't seem to be letting up at all and appeared to be getting progressively worse, I began to panic on a whole other level, to the point that I shifted into another spiritual reality, realizing that I was not in control and that there was a strong chance I might die.

I then had this very calm, peaceful voice come in, and it said to me, "this could be your time, and maybe you should prepare yourself to let go." So, I began a harrowing ritual that I will never forget. I made a very deliberate decision to consciously "let go," and I started crying to myself as I was thinking about my family. I then sent out my heartfelt wishes to all of them and got under my desk to wait for the inevitable.

I heard someone yell, "Run, run, run!" It was Frank, he was yelling at me to run, as there was a sudden break. So with that, my adrenaline kicked in, and I quickly made my way to the door, and I flew down those stairs to the streets below, feeling like I had wings on my feet. It was surreal.

Once down the stairs, I went outside onto the street, and my voice said, "Wow, this is like being in a bad Hollywood movie." It was just as dangerous as it was inside. The earth beneath us was still rumbling and shaking, and we also had to contend with the debris and glass falling down on us from the surrounding high-rise buildings.

I waited long enough to see that all my co-workers had gotten out of our building. Then I supported and guided anyone in the streets to stay safe by walking in the middle of the road towards the T intersection 1,000 meters away at the top of Hereford Street. Once we all arrived, we peeled off and went our separate ways.

I then frantically tried to ring my family, but there was no reception as the towers were all down. I calmed myself down and began to walk out of town. I felt safer on the streets and kept myself as safe as possible until I came across another very devastating sight!

As I was heading out of town, I noticed to the left that the Pyne Gould Guinness building, a historic five-story building, had billows of dust everywhere. It had pancaked itself to the ground. Yet again, I jolted back into that scary otherworldly place again, and all I could do was carry on walking while silently sobbing as I wiped tears from my eyes. I survived the Christchurch earthquake of 2011.

On Tuesday, February 22, 2011, at 12.51 p.m., a Mw6.2 earthquake struck Christchurch at a depth of 6.7 kilometers south-east of Christchurch in the South Island of New Zealand. There were 185 deaths and 1,500-2000 injuries, 164 of which were serious. My heartfelt condolences go out to all the Christchurch families affected by this disaster.

~ You're Slipping Through the Cracks ~

"You're slipping through the cracks but falling into openings. That certain person. A remarkable thing. The sudden event, A season of hardship. Being diagnosed. Falling in and out of love. An intense phase of feeling lost. Or the death that stopped the clocks and shook your world...

Something dropped you to your knees, only to pick you up again and thrust you into an unexpected entrance of a life-changing Opening.

An Opening where everyday existence and the core of your being collapse into one, and nothing feels the same again. You are not being neglected, not being ignored. Instead, a great spirit speaks to you. A conversation between this source and your soul is significant and ongoing. It had always been. But you can hear it much clearer since passing through the Opening.

Listen, it reveals: The strength of your connection is just as powerful as the sun.

You are awesomely comprised of wisdom and creation. You are not alone but guided by intuition.

And while on earth, you are a complete universe, holding a continuance of profound experiences with spiritual meaning."
~Susan Frybort~

The Aftermath of the Earthquakes

I began walking out of town towards Manchester Street to check on Shannon. When I got there, I discovered that Shan was okay and that she had walked to the family home in Richmond. I continued to walk home myself, and when I arrived, I saw that Daniel, my youngest, was also okay as he had stayed home that day. I then needed to check on Joshua, Lena, and Noah. I eventually got through to them on the phone, and they were also fine. I then asked Lena if I could borrow her car so I could check up on my sister Ingrid and her family close by. Driving to my sister's house was a mission and a half.

The roads were in a terrible state as liquefaction and water had bubbled up from underground. The water on the road could look very deceptive, as it could be hiding a sinkhole, and I came across cars that had been taken by a sinkhole. So, I decided to watch the other drivers in front of me go through the water, and if they got to the other side safely, I would follow the exact path they took. I was able to navigate my way around the streets like this till I got to my sister's. Once there, I found out she and her family were safe and well.

The next phase for me as a manager was to check in on all our families around Christchurch, and we did this by either checking on them face to face or by ringing them. We then allocated the family caseloads according to proximity. I was closer to town, and I continued to work alongside those families, and Izzy was allocated the families who were located closer to her on the other side of town. We then assessed all our families' needs and arranged supplies, food, water, or whatever for them through our networks. Some of my families were in the "Red Zone," the areas policed heavily by the armed forces. These were the zones in and around the center of Christchurch that had sustained the most damage. Anyone who entered the Red Zones had to get clearance to proceed through the barriers. So, if I needed to check in on my families, I had to state my intentions to the officials, and then I'd be allowed to pass through the barriers.

For the first week or so after the earthquakes, you couldn't flush your toilets or drink from any of the taps. I had to dig a long drop in the garden out in the back and create a makeshift toilet surrounded by a tarpaulin for privacy. Gathering five and ten-liter water containers also became a necessity, as you would have to line up on the streets and sometimes wait for up to two hours in a queue to fill up your containers at the water trucks.

Izzy and I continued to help our families through this crisis by supporting them emotionally and by offering them ongoing day to day support as required. Eventually, we had a chance to relocate to another local office space with another local organization, the Linwood Community Centre. They offered us a lovely little office space in a quaint old character house they were using. So, we moved in with them and shared this space with these two lovely ladies for some time. Over time, we all became good friends, and sometimes we would go down to the trivia nights at the local pub to have a few drinks and chill out. It was lovely to now be around other like-minded colleagues who also worked in the community.

~ The Life you Want to Grow ~

"The Life you want to grow into will ask you to gather and reclaim ingredients you may have lost along the way.

Your voice, your truth, your choice, your bravery, your boundaries, and your care. Learn to recognize these things, find them and gather them from your heart and belly. With these ingredients of inner power held strongly in your being, you can grow towards a life more attuned with your heart."
~Brigit Anna McNeill~

A Phoenix Rising From the Ashes

I would say that this life-changing event was what I would call my "tower moment," and my life changed drastically after it. Before the earthquake, I wasn't really living on my terms at all. I was happy with my professional life, but I wasn't satisfied with my personal life.

So, to fully understand my story, I will go back to the beginning. So, I'm the oldest of seven children, and I grew up in Bishopdale in Christchurch. I have so many happy memories of my family growing up in my neighborhood. Every school holiday, we would all go raspberry and strawberry picking to get pocket money over Christmas time. All the families knew each other back then, and we all went to the same schools. So, I grew up with a strong sense of family and community, which was always a strong foundation for me growing up.

As I look back, I can also see that the loss of my mother due to mental illness and alcohol at the age of four impacted me significantly. As a child, I found that not having a mum to turn to for nurturing and advice was very difficult. From an early age, I remember feeling a sense of shame around the way my mum had left, and then I questioned my self-worth as her oldest daughter. I can see I was in the beginning stages of developing childhood trauma, and I was struggling in a few areas that would play out later in my life. I wouldn't ask for what I needed, I would repress my genuine emotions, I wouldn't talk about how I felt, I feared being vulnerable, I sometimes had a hard time trusting others, and I was afraid to say no for fear of disappointing people.

I had a few relationships throughout my teenage years and into my early 20s. Nothing of significance came up for me with my relationships until I met that one partner. So, when I met him, I felt like I was falling in love with him, but maybe I was falling in love with the idea of settling down and having a family. They say that you experience three types of love in your lifetime. This was an example of the second type of love. It's called "Hard Love," and you will learn the hard lessons from it. In this relationship, I experienced other types of trauma. I can see that when I was in this type of relationship, I hadn't learned enough discernment about how to choose the right partner for me. In this type of relationship, you can inadvertently choose a narcissist, which was bound to happen to me as I'm the exact opposite of that personality type. I'm an empath. I remember feeling as if I just had to hang in there as that's just what you do. But, in the end, the relationship became too compromising for me, so I walked away.

When I eventually discovered that I was an empath, I learned much about the amazing traits I have. I found out that I am pretty sensitive, I can usually read people quite well, I'm a very peaceful and calm person, I don't like drama, I have a very eclectic taste in music, I love animals and nature, I can pick up on vibes in a room, I can be a daydreamer, I can be very quirky and creative, I'm very kind and compassionate, I'm a good listener, I'm very free-spirited, and I need my alone time to re-energize myself.

After the earthquake, I began to reassess every aspect of my life and began to make some profound changes. I was offered a chance to move to Brisbane, Australia, in 2012, and when I first arrived, I was able to return to working in the community sector, which has always been familiar to me.

It's so interesting that after all this time working in the community sector, and in the mental health sector specifically for the past eight years, I have now been able to gain a deeper perspective as to why my mother may have struggled with her mental illness. She was a young mum and from what I know now, I realize that I needed to be more gentle on both myself and her. Now I'm more at peace with both myself and my mum, and I know deep down in my heart that she is proud of me.

So as you read my story, you can learn a lot about who I am, where I come from, and my journey and maybe get an idea of where I'm heading, and if I was to summarise my life's journey so far, I would say that I am now okay about all of the good and bad times that I've gone through because they were all lessons and they gave me a greater appreciation for my life.

I might have had regrets in the past, but that was because I didn't know myself, how I felt or how to fix myself. Now I don't feel any of those conflicting emotions anymore. I've made my peace with myself, making sure to stay in the flow of life and live in the moment as much as possible without regrets. I wrote this story to share a part of my life with you in the hope that you may realise that transformation and hope is always possible no matter what you go through in life. My intention is that you may also find a type of meaning from my journey to support you on yours.

"Unless knowledge is transformed into wisdom and wisdom is expressed in character; education is a wasteful process."

~ Sai Baba

CHAPTER NINE

―――⊸∘◯∾◯∘⊶―――

A Journey of Self

By Jenny Bot

It's summer 2022, and it's lovely here in Central California. But let's start our journey in 1981 when I was born in California, USA. Life – for me, at least – is like a roller coaster with lots of ups and downs. I am an only child in a San Francisco suburb, that I have a lot to be grateful for. Growing up in California gave me a distinct appreciation for all cultures and beliefs. As a huge melting pot of new and first-generation immigrants, the San Francisco Bay Area is one of the most dynamic places to live in the world, and I had the privilege of growing up with a group of friends from diverse backgrounds and perspectives. My family history is very diverse as well; I grew up with healthy debate as the norm at the dinner table, which taught me that it's OK to disagree with the people you love.

As a child, my interests were animals, nature, plants, and science – and not much has changed. I am still a nature girl who loves gardening and dogs. But that is about where the peace begins and ends. For 35 years, I've lived a life of go go go, not knowing what a break meant.

I started working in the family business at eight years old. After I got home from school, my dad would be waiting for me. "Jenny," he would say, "are you ready?" My dad ran a vending business. He wasn't a large man, but his biceps were. His overall presence was serious and intimidating, but he was quick to joke around and laugh. He had a contagious smile and curious spirit.

OK, Dad, let me just drop off my backpack here in the corner. I've done my homework."

Yes, I could walk or ride my bike two blocks to school and back. The walk was the most peaceful part of my day. To and from school, I would pass by the neighbor's roses and the barking dogs. I would literally stop to smell every pretty flower, carefully cross a very busy intersection on my own, and arrive at school, sometimes drenched from the California winter rains. The way home was no better or worse, the hot days mitigated by the tree-lined streets. Old cars with their huge gas nozzles blowing in my face. Other kids, all walking in different directions, were the norm.

I would arrive home sweaty and ready for a break, but there was always something to do. My chores included but weren't limited to dishes, laundry, making dinner, vacuuming, general dusting, tidying, and pulling weeds. I was always washing the cars, motorcycles, trucks, and boats we owned. I was my dad's right hand, his only child, so I learned things normally taught to boys too. Handing him the right tool, helping him change the oil, the son he never had.

As an only child, I never felt like I couldn't do things, and my dad made sure of one thing: he talked to me about science, physics, math, and mechanics and instilled excitement in me. He loved coming into my room in the middle of the night to wake me up to do science experiments. His favorite experiment would have us run our feet on the carpet in the dark, then stick our fingers together to create a blue line of electricity. It gave me a certain wonder and curiosity about other unseen things. He was also into ham radios, so we had a huge antenna on our house. There was never really a boring moment or a break. Weekends as a kid were full of trips to the lake or Sacramento delta to go boating. Or daily bike rides strapped to the back of his Harley Davidson up to the hills of Skyline Boulevard or Half Moon Bay. We, on the outside, were a happy family, very active in the community.

Every weekday I would help him with the vending business. The sounds of the coins filling up the rolls. Taking the rolls to the bank. Lifting tray after tray of heavy cans of soda, chips, and candy from the wholesaler to the truck. Unloading it onto dollies at each location, we would go from San Jose to San Francisco on our routes filling up the vending machines, collecting the coins, repeat.

The people are the thing I remember the most about each location, from workers at the run of the mill office buildings to the retirement home, where all the old ladies would pinch my cheeks. Sometimes it seems like just yesterday, but I haven't seen my father in over six years, may he rest in peace. Honestly, I have more terrible memories of my parents fighting, but I don't want to dwell on those. But that kind of relentless activity is what I mean when I say it was 35 years before I could relax. I was born into a family that was always GO GO GO. My mother is a beautiful woman with grace and style. She is very caring towards those she loves. She is fiercely independent and worked full-time, so I saw her less, and when I did, she was often very stressed. I understand now, as a mother of three, how demanding a family life can be. I look around at all the seemingly happy people and wonder if they ever felt like I did. Anxiety ruled my life for 35 years; I felt as though I was constantly in a battle against gravity. How do you go from such pressure to true peace?

Although they were filled with constant activity, the first 16 years of my life were somewhat idyllic. I was a 4.0 GPA student in all my Advanced Placement courses. I was smart, I worked hard, and my future was looking bright. I tested into high-level courses and started college at 16, my junior year of high school. I was so excited about the prospect of graduating with a science degree early from a good college, possibly on an academic scholarship.

But the unforeseen sometimes happens. In the year 2000, when I was meant to graduate high school and start college full-time, a car accident where I was rear-ended on the freeway changed everything. I was only 17, and that also meant I couldn't work my job at the local coffee shop as a barista. I was completely reliant on my family for help. This was the time I needed to be independent, but the same year, my parents divorced. My life after the car accident looked completely different. Everything suffered, my relationships, my income, my health.

I had lingering pain from the accident; no one could figure out what it was. I went to doctor after doctor looking for answers. I had been a healthy girl working at a grocery store as a bagger, and I was lifting weights at the gym, but I had to give up because my back would seize up as pain shot down my leg, like I was reliving the car accident over and over. But according to every scan, I was OK.

It never rains, but it pours. Just like that, my perfect-seeming life wasn't looking so perfect. I had to grow up in what felt like overnight. Everything changed. I had taken my simple routine for granted: school, work, home, studying, and repeat. Suddenly I was getting Fs at school, and that consistency and support I had were gone. And then, just when I thought, OK, maybe I can come back from this, on my 18th birthday, my mother left to remarry, and I was left on my own to figure it all out. Not what I thought my life would look like. Two years earlier, I was on track for a scholarship to a big university, but I would now go to study at a community college.

I needed guidance during this period in my life, but I had none. I went back to work, still in pain, kept going to college, and brought my grades up. However, that year of failure is still on my permanent college record (I did finally get my Baccalaureate in Biology. It just took a few extra years and a semester in Italy), and it affected my job prospects with my GPA never being able to get those years back. Things in my personal life weren't looking any better – I was in an abusive relationship from age 15-20 with an alcoholic, cheating boyfriend that took me years to be able to financially leave. The mysterious back pain lasted for three years. I was going to every kind of doctor you could imagine, and there was no physical explanation for these sharp, shooting pains down my back and legs that would come out of nowhere.

Eventually, after years of no one being able to tell me what was wrong with me, I saw an osteopath. He basically gave me homeopathic medicine and talked to me about how I was feeling. He got me on anxiety medication that seemed to help my overall outlook, and in our sessions, he would just hold his hand over me like he was praying. I was so desperate I thought, OK, this person is crazy, but at that point, I would have done just about anything to get the pain to go away. And so I lay there allowing him perform what looked like voodoo to me because I truly wanted to go back to living my normal life, working without pain and supporting myself.

I'm still not sure if he really did anything or not, but what I do know is the pain slowly started going away after each session. Until one day, something incredible happened. I was laying there on the table, and I was able to talk through and let go of all my fears, my horrible fear of death and the dread that constantly followed me around. And on the other side of all that fear was overwhelming love engulfing my body. Beautiful feelings came over me like a wave. I was euphoric. For twenty minutes, I was in a state of complete bliss. I left confused by what had happened.

I went back the next week, upset, and I confronted him.

I said, "What did you do to me?!"

He seemed perplexed. "I didn't do anything to you, you did it to yourself," he said.

I thought: Is my own mind that powerful?

I said, "I don't believe you."

OK," he said, "I'll explain it. Most people don't have the experience you did, but since you did, it's only fair. Our mind is that powerful. You can connect with the source of all creation and that love you felt is always around if you let yourself feel it."

That's incredible," I said, but in my heart, I knew it was true. We all hold the power inside ourselves, our fear blocks it out. I always knew I had "gifts," but until now, I didn't know that on the other side of all that, fear and forgiveness was overwhelming, pure love and joy.

You can't plan for everything, but you can forgive yourself and adapt. There is always a silver lining just waiting to be found. I can't forget all the teachers that cheered me on. I remember all the friends that listened to my pain and my family that sent me money when I needed it. Little things go a long way to a person struggling just to get by day by day financially, emotionally, and spiritually.

I must say my father's mother, who is turning 96-years-old in just a few days, has been a huge inspiration to me, and at that time in my life, she reached out to me many times to help. She never wanted to see anyone suffer. She bailed me out more than once. Her new husband helped me too. The little things started to add up.

You must take action to change your future, and that's just what I did. I slowly rebuilt my life with the help of family and new friends.

In 2002, after recovering from my injury, I studied a semester of college in Italy. Italy was a huge turning point for me. I had been a serious student growing up, and now I had this freedom in a whole new country, with new people and new experiences. For once, I wasn't really focused on learning or school, I immersed myself in the culture, language, food, and people.

BOOM BOOM BOOM – the music you can feel in your soul until 10 am on a Wednesday morning with the sun so bright as I stumbled out of the nightclub still drunk. Everyone was so beautiful. I remember thinking: I'm not much over five feet tall, and everyone around me looks like a supermodel. Not only that, but everyone was so open sexually, I mean men with men, women with women, and trans women that would make your head turn twice – stunningly beautiful people everywhere. It was like a dream, art, culture, and ambiance you can't imagine, the smell of a 500-year-old building decorated to the nines, and the air was just different. And everyone on ecstasy, which was literally like candy in the early 2000s, the club life, the party culture; I was fully immersed for six months of craziness. I would say I needed to get this out of my system, to see how other people lived, to see things from a different perspective. And when I came back to California, I had a whole new appreciation for the opportunities many Americans take for granted.

My family came to America generations ago, pursuing the dream of a better life. Now, with this new perspective, I felt an obligation to honor the sacrifices they had made just to give me the chance at a happy life.

In 2005 I graduated college with a Bachelorette in Biology, a dream I worked hard to achieve. I moved up to Northern California to finish my university and focus on myself and study. Then the loneliness got to me, and after years without a serious relationship, I got engaged to a new man. Unfortunately, the man I was engaged to became incredibly abusive after I moved in with him. I really thought he was going to kill me, and once we had moved in together, it was incredibly hard to leave. I spent two years with him in silence, not to mention the life I had imagined when I graduated. I wanted to live my life, but instead, I was again back to the drawing board again, just trying to survive. I had given myself up once again to someone that wanted to control me, and when I did finally leave, I had to start over yet again.

But I am a hopeless romantic. When I met my first husband in 2006, it was a whirlwind romance. He was a tall man, around 6'5," and was wearing a kilt. He had a huge personality to match his presence – he was always quick to smile and didn't take things too seriously. He was kind in spirit and would give away his last dollar to someone on the street or even his shirt. I met him at a casino at a poker table. I had worked at the casino for nearly a year and would play as much as I could on nights off. This was one of those nights off, but it was different. We talked so much that we both lost the poker game. We hung out after the game and talked all night about philosophy and life. We both had deep wells of passion we wanted to share; meeting each other felt like finding a light in the darkness of closed-off people. We didn't want to be apart, and for the next decade, we weren't. In 2008 we eloped.

In 2009 we moved, got a house together, and we played more than anything. We had so many wonderful adventures, traveling all over California and Nevada. We eloped in Reno, Nevada, and shortly after moved to Las Vegas. We started gardening, a spiritual meetup group, and Yoga with a master teacher. I felt like up until I met him, I had focused on my mind, and in this part of my life, I was able to learn about my body and spiritual growth. Being a better person, learning, and helping others were the cornerstones of our relationship.

But behind the fun façade, there was a darkness coming that neither of us could have anticipated. His bipolar disorder was undiagnosed until it was too late, and alcohol combined with mental illness is a recipe for disaster. I didn't know he was suicidal, but he had a plan that didn't involve me. Losing him was the most devastating moment in my life. Everything changed.

You don't know how strong you are till you are challenged. You can never tell what seeds of a new life will grow from a tragedy like that, but something will come if you remain unafraid and never take the little things for granted.

It was 2016. My father had also taken his life by suicide just three months before my husband. I decided to move back to California to start over. It had taken years to build my life with my first husband, but after he died, I moved and lost contact with everything familiar except my three-year-old daughter.

My beautiful daughter was born in 2012 at home in Las Vegas. Her birth was planned with the midwife, and it was an incredible experience. She came late at 42 weeks but was very strong and healthy. I felt so grateful and lucky to be a mom. My daughter's laugh, her cries, and her need for me to be strong are what kept me going in the darkest times. I knew from my experience that she needed consistency from me. She required me not to give up.

So, I moved back to California to a quiet house on an island.

I needed peace above all other things to put what happened into perspective and find a way on. I was so angry at my husband for making that choice. The anger was paralyzing. I just wanted a second chance that I felt would never come. I didn't understand why, but it was a complete shock to my emotional system. I had a really hard time accepting that my daughter would grow up without knowing her father, and that we would never get to talk to him again. So I moved close to family; my beautiful mother was just a few houses down. After losing my father, I wanted to be close to her. The idea that loss could happen to anyone you love at any time puts a priority on relationships you cherish. So, I focused on what I had, not what I didn't. The memories of the people you love never leave you, so make more. Don't be afraid to have difficult conversations; often, they help you grow closer to the people you care about. We often get caught up in our daily routines and forget to say how we feel, or we are too afraid to express those feelings. Letting go of anger and fear was essential for growth and happiness. Once I was able to let go of fear and anger, my life got a whole lot better. Suddenly I didn't feel anxious and stressed all the time.

The biggest tragedy is feeling alone, not wanting to burden others with our issues. But we must reach out to each other. None of us asked to be here, but we can make the best of it while we are.

We don't have to suffer alone. You can create a better future for yourself and those around you. It's in your hands. My relationship with my father was rocky, but I miss him so much.

A huge part of my healing came from going to a grief group for suicide survivors, where I learned to ask for help, something I had been afraid to do for so long. Social connections are essential for growth. So, I refocused my attention on interpersonal relationships. This meant everyone currently in my life and reaching out to start making new friends with similar interests. My life was much different now, with a four-year-old daughter and twins on the way.

I had never felt relaxed in my life, not once in 35 years leading up to the moment I lost fifty pounds in one day.

The Birth

The table is cold and flat, the lights blaring – almost like an alien abduction scene out of a sci-fi movie, only this is happening. The doctors make the first cut. Gathered around me are nurses, waiting, ready. Suddenly a cry, my husband leaning over me. I see a tear in his eye. It's our first son being born; they show him to me over the curtain. He looks fat and angry, he isn't warm anymore, and they quickly take him to the incubator to warm him and wipe off all the fluid. His cry warms my heart as I know he is a strong boy, but I knew this already; carrying him for the last 38 weeks has been an incredible journey just to get to this moment of joy.

Paralyzed on the table, all I could do was watch, almost as if I was just a witness to this extraordinary event. And then, after some struggling, I heard the second cry out; our second son was born four minutes later. He was a little more stubborn than his brother, but I have done it, delivered full-term twins with a healthy pregnancy at the age of 35, what the doctors had considered high risk, and advanced age, and we are all healthy. This is the most joyous moment of my life, and all I can do is be grateful, after all the fear that I have lived through, to see them now running around at five years old happy, joyful, playful, smart young boys. My children are my greatest joy in life.

The most important thing (and it has taken many setbacks to teach me this) is to not give up. For me, the motivation to keep going has been my children. My daughter is now nearly ten years old, and the twins are five, but when my eldest was just a baby, in my darker moments, I would look at her face and push myself to do better for her sake. That motivation hasn't diminished. Instead, it drives me to those little moments of joy we get. It's impossible to be sad in the presence of my children. You don't get a day off to sulk when you have kids. You get up and feed them, care for them, and in turn, they distract you from negative thoughts. They give you something to focus on other than yourself or pity. You find the strength you didn't know you had inside because you must.

In 2018, I married my second husband. A second chance is a beautiful miracle I don't take for granted. We had all our friends and family at this grand event. It took me a long time to get to this moment, but it was all worth it.

Adding not only the twins to our family in 2017 but also my now beautiful husband. He is such a magnetic soul, caring and thoughtful. He makes me feel safe and supported. His parents also were right there for us, helping with the kids and a huge part of the healing process. After all that turmoil, it took a long time of communication, but I now feel relaxed. I had PTSD for a time after the suicide, with nightmares every night for a year. But one day, they stopped, and I finally quit punishing myself and allowed myself enjoy the three beautiful children we get to raise and each other.

My second husband I have known since freshman year of high school. In fact, we grew up on the same street. We have been friends for years, and it has been comforting that he knew my father growing up, as we have so many fun childhood memories we can share together. He also knew my first husband, which has made it easier for me – I had a lot less to explain about what had happened since he already knew most of it. I am so grateful for peace in my life, the little things I can enjoy so much more with love. I know my father and first husband would be so happy for us.

Now I am living life, experiencing happiness that so many don't get to experience, and I know it's not forever, but each moment can feel like an eternity. I fall asleep fast at the end of the night without worrying about the future so much, just enjoying each day to the fullest. I know we don't get to live forever, but I want to live a life of meaning where I help and care for others.

My most tight-knit community for years was and still is poker, from playing when I lived in Las Vegas to online play today. In 2019 I started full-time streaming on Twitch. It's been thousands of hours as a mod and now a live streamer of my own for nearly four years. I have a ton of healing that has been done through all the friendships I have made and connections with other people from all over the world. After having to start all over with new friends, I am so grateful for each relationship.

We must find the time for ourselves to grow, learn, play, and enjoy being human.

It must come from within. Your desire and your vision must be clear-the clearer, the better. Write down your goals for your life, this decade, this year, this month, this week, this day, this hour, this minute. What is it your heart is telling you? And think bigger – we sell ourselves too short. Don't listen to negativity and don't ask why not. Break down your goals into smaller steps until you see a clear path to get there. I hope my story inspires you to transform the negative aspects of your life into wisdom.

What now? I was excited when I agreed to write my part in this book. There have been many challenges in my life, I am sharing my story to inspire you to do anything you want. Don't let your current circumstances hold you back from what could be. We continue to be faced with challenges throughout our lives, but it's the use we turn those challenges to what really matters. I enjoy sharing, sometimes oversharing, but it feels better because I know you are reading this because you want to, because some part of you is looking for answers. Just know the answers are already inside you. Search your heart.

Sending Love to You.

PS: Get to know yourself; it's the greatest journey waiting for you right now.

I recommend a book that helped me along the way, *Personal Power Through Awareness* by Sanaya Roman.

"The wound is the place where the light enters you."

~ Rumi

CHAPTER TEN

---∞◦⌒∾◦∾---

Calibrating My Heart, My Mind, My Soul and My Truth

By Sonja Anastasia

In the 70's I was born into a family in conflict. My mother was afraid and my grandparents did not want my mother to have me. They despised my father because he was not of the right race, accent, religion, and culture. My father turned out to be an extremely abusive man and my mother left him shortly after I was born. My biological father's abuse and my mother's separation from her family left my father in total despair.

My mother's circumstances left her in a state of anguish. The trauma she endured made her bitter, resentful, and angry. At this point, she had no love left in her heart to care for and nurture a child.

My mom set a lot of blame for her life on my shoulders. Every time I spoke, she would go into a fit of rage until I was silent. I felt as if I were forbidden to speak. Every time she screamed, I would feel tense, like I could not breathe. As a child, I didn't understand how to communicate my needs or feelings. I felt was that everything was my fault. It became my responsibility to take care of her by managing her emotions and behaving well. Early on, I was conscious about never disappointing my mother so I wouldn't receive negative attention. I walked on eggshells never receiving any primary care, needs, or love being met by my mother. I longed to be seen and heard.

My mother was always seeking a way out of being a single mother, and she began drinking. This only increased her anger, rage, shouting and screaming. Her lack of presence to fully show up in my life caused me deep feelings of abandonment, rejection, pain and sadness. These feelings haunted me into my adult life and spilled into my relationships.

I learned early on, "Good girls are seen and not heard." I had no siblings to learn from and my mother often passed me off to my babysitter so she wouldn't have to deal with me. My babysitter was terrific; she took my mother under her wing and began teaching her how to be a mother and care for me. My grandmother had not come back into the picture yet. My mother needed guidance and support. She received this from my babysitter. My babysitter and I had a special relationship filled with love, nurturing and care until she passed away in 2012.

When I was three years old, the stress from the verbal and physical abuse took a toll on my physical well-being. My stomach had been distended for days. My babysitter kept telling my mother that I was complaining of a stomachache. Once again, my mother ignored it. Finally, my babysitter insisted to my mother this wouldn't go away on its own and that she should take me to the hospital. My mother said no, it's not necessary; it will go away.

But my babysitter insisted on taking me to the hospital. Once at the hospital, the doctors couldn't figure out what was wrong. At this point, my skin color changed, and I became very ill. My stomachache persisted into a fourth day and the doctors at the hospital ran more tests on me with renewed urgency.

Finally, the doctors discovered that I had a ruptured appendix. I was immediately prepped for an invasive surgery. Due to my size the surgeon would have to cut open my abdomen. The impact of the surgery took a toll on my body, and I ended up in a coma. The situation, at best, looked bleak. The doctors told my mother and family that it would be a miracle if I woke up without brain damage.

The good news was my grandparents came around during this time and started becoming a part of my life. My grandmother arranged for the priest to come pray over me. She would speak to me, pray, and show me love until one day I woke up. The doctors were in absolute disbelief. They did several brain scans to ensure my brain was functioning properly. After many tests, it was declared that I received a miracle "gift of life back from God." Nothing made sense to any of the doctors. As I grew older and was told this story, I believed it was the power of my grandmother's and babysitter's love that healed me back to life. I also felt God and his Angels spared my too.

After I was released from the hospital, my grandmother began taking a more active role in my life. We developed a special heart-to-heart relationship. She picked me up every weekend, giving me space from my mother. My grandmother showered me with love by teaching me things like cooking, gardening, cleaning, restoring used furniture, listening to music, reading, and anything she was involved in. Every day, I still feel, see and know in my heart, our time together was the most precious gift God has given me. Her presence in my life was healing and balanced me to wholeness after enduring so much trauma. I prayed and wished my mother would have changed her behavior after I nearly died. Sadly, she only got worse in her addiction with each passing year.

Due to my mother's addiction, I grew up in different families from different cultures. So, early on I learned the mechanics of surviving in various environments and continuously adjusted myself to being the quiet good girl no matter the conditions, and this eventually became a pattern of people pleasing. I didn't want to disappoint anyone, so I stuffed my emotions which left me feeling scared and alone in the world. I continued this pattern as a means of self protection.

A few years later, I began going to school and was extremely excited about this new beginning. I faced many challenges at school due to my inability to communicate effectively with my teachers and peers. Using my voice was not the norm in my household. Why would I speak up at school? In school, I would have to be forced to speak. Deep down, I felt if I spoke, I would get in trouble, be a disappointment, and be yelled at. So, it was best to be quiet like I learned at home to survive the conditions.

I did my schoolwork and got good grades but never really engaged with teachers or other students. I was highly introverted and fearful of disappointing everyone. Being an only child living in a not-so-good neighborhood, I got picked on and beaten up a lot. This only kept reinforcing my wounds, fearing disappointment and not being loved. These were now woven into my entire being energetically day by day, feeling there was no way out.

In the '80s, my grandmother passed, and I missed her so much. I missed our weekends together, and I missed her love. I missed her presence. The time of her passing was pivotal. Even now, I could not express how I felt about her dying. It was the first time I felt my heart shatter so profoundly. I felt like I had lost a grandma, mom, and best friend all at once. Even when I asked what happened? I would be screamed at and told that kids don't get to ask these questions.

My mother, at this point, felt that since her mother had passed, there was no reason for her to stay in New York. Furthermore, she had no relationship with anyone else in the family. So one day, she picked us up and moved us to Hawaii. At first, I was distraught that the little world I had in terms of family, friends, or love would now be gone. In addition, I lived most of my elementary school days in my energetic body. Learning behaviors to survive instead of having a childhood like most kids full of fun, play, joy, and happiness.

My mother only got a studio apartment once we arrived in Hawaii. We slept next to one another with no space for me to retreat from her verbal abuse.

I felt isolated again without any support except once a week, speaking on the phone or writing letters to friends and family. About three months after we moved, feeling my way around in a new environment, I faced many challenging adjustments. But I also began to see that a way of living happy was genuinely possible.

I began making friends and we would go to the beach together. They would teach me how to bodyboard and surf. I felt free being in the ocean. I loved the water and everything about being on the beach. More importantly, the beach was a haven for me to retreat from my mother's wrath. My mother never learned to swim and despised the heat and the sand. I felt I finally found a place where I could find peace within myself.

Hawaii would be a new chapter in my life, where I learned the true meaning of love for other's lives and family. The word "Aloha," in essence, means love. I desired to feel love in my home, and I felt it continuously around me now living in this new culture. My friends became like family to me and loved me unconditionally. We supported one another. Hawaiian culture, values and beliefs are centered around treating everyone like family. The word for family in Hawaiian is "Ohana."

My friend's mothers accepted me with grace, ease and love. It felt great to receive motherly love. Finally, I knew what it meant to be part of a family where looking after one another was a normal way of living. I felt secure, guided and protected in my surroundings. Life was great, and Hawaii was a chapter in my life that will always serve as one of the best places I have ever lived. I was able to explore, open my heart and consciousness. I am still connected to most of the friends I made in Hawaii 25 years later. Once you befriend a Hawaiian, you are friends for life. Such a beautiful culture filled with great core values and beliefs.

As I was in my twenties, I continued to live life in a flash. I kept asking myself why I was here. What does going through all of this in life mean? I never had conversations about life with my mother. It appeared that everyone around me figured out something about the energetic flow of life I missed. Life felt very hard, and I lived in so much fear it was choking me from the inside. Fear of disappointing everyone, fear of abandonment, fear of rejection, fear of not being loved, fear and continuous feelings of not being worthy, fear of being discarded if I spoke up since my home life was not good. My outside relationships became a source of comfort and strength. These relational patterns running in me created an extreme people pleaser and co-dependent pattern to the point that I lost track of who I was as a woman.

In my twenties I started doing some soul-searching, reading personal development books, reading the Bible, and praying to God. My relationship with God, listening to my intuition, sound healing, somatic therapy, yoga, meditating and journaling would become valuable tools to start healing myself from childhood trauma. When I was searching and applying these tools, I was not fully aware that I was on a path to healing myself, except when I reflect on my mid-twenties. This period was a turning point. Now it has turned into a lifelong pursuit in the healing arts and coaching to align others to their inner vision, find their purpose and lead life by heart's desire. Helping myself helps others become better versions of themselves and this trickles down to ever person they interact with. I intend to serve many more people, for the rest of my lifetime, and I am truly getting started.

I've learned from various metaphysical and personal development teachers, books, and seminars. I heard phrases such as "your parents did their best with the resources they had at the time," "forgiveness heals you, not them," and to be "grateful every day."

Honestly, it took me time to wrap my head around the context of these concepts. I learned along the way that I needed to explore ways I could unpack the years of trauma endured. I needed to release my anger, bitterness and resentment so I could fully understand the true meaning of these teachings to live life fully expressed in wholeness.

Honestly, at the beginning of my journey it all made no sense in my mind. Nevertheless, I continued down the path. I began meditating, journaling and writing gratitude daily. As I continued developing practices of being observant and consistent in my embodiment, I grew deep compassion for myself and others. I began fully accepting everything received in my life. Peeling back the layers gave me tremendous clarity. When I fully understood forgiveness and gratitude I was able to make the shift and understand that my parents did their best with the knowledge, and resources they had at the time.

Furthermore, I discovered we are all created in the divine image of God or the Creator. Therefore, it's truly every person's birthright to feel and know that they are worthy and loved. Once this sank in my heart, mind, and soul, I released all the fears I had been carrying around. I began to make sense of everything which made no sense previously. As a result, I began to transform myself and my own life entirely.

I started to be mindful of my words, thoughts, and actions. I reconciled every previous occurrence in my mind by repatterning my thoughts around each event. Once I did that, I was able to release all my expectations of who I thought she needed to be as a mom. These small practices became so liberating. I started to feel this aliveness, happiness, and joy in my heart all the time instead of the victim's state of mind and being. Even though my upbringing was filled with events of abuse and trauma, I learned that once I empowered myself to change my perception, everything I knew or thought became alive in this new way of being. As a result, I felt great about my childhood, truly blessed and grateful for everything.

I learned that it truly takes a village to raise a child. So many loving people crossed my path. My babysitter, grandmother, and friend's mothers all invested their time, care and love into me. I still feel deeply grateful for all of them being there for me. Also, I learned the gift of diversity in my early years by being around different families and cultures. This helped guide my communication and connection skills by giving me the confidence to effortlessly form relationships with others. Finally, I have a big heart and deep love for people for who they truly are in their hearts. These are a few of the greatest gifts life has given me, which still serves me in being the empathetic woman that I am today.

My final test in releasing my former patterns of fear of disappointment came in 2018. I suddenly received the news that my mother was on life support. Once I received the call, I boarded a plane to Colorado, where she lived at the time. I spoke to her weekly, and I was not even aware she was sick and had not seen her for a few years before she passed.

I felt a little nervous, seeing her face to face and knowing she was dying. I felt like this could be my chance to finally let it all go, finally have a voice to tell her how I truly felt after all these years. But, once I arrived in Colorado, everything changed in my heart, and I did so much personal healing. I began to feel it was an honor and privilege to help her feel peace in her heart during this time. Once I set the intention to help her transition peacefully, every person, place and thing around me stepped in my path to support me.

For starters, the hotel I originally booked didn't have my reservation, so I was moved to the hotel down the street. When the woman brought me to my room, the story of Jesus in pictures was on the walls. A divine sign. Next, I went to the hospital and met with the doctor. The doctor told me not to be alarmed, but that she hadn't moved in ten days and was lifeless. I entered her room slowly. You see, the bond between a child and a parent is so strong even though she had not moved; I am here now, and she will wake up and move. The doctor looked confused when I told her this, but she went along.

I entered the room and went behind her bed while the doctor was in front of the bed. My mother's body began to wake up. She started moving. The doctor looked at me in complete shock. I sensed right away that transitioning her to hospice would happen soon. I also knew we would speak when the time was right. My mother was restless, angry, and bitter even in her passing. I was by her side when she woke up and realized it was me. Although she started yelling at me like when I was a small child, I remained quiet. I felt her fear of dying, and her suffering. I felt her lack of connection to herself.

I had compassion for her. When I was a child, I would freeze and feel fear of disappointing her. Later that evening, I asked myself what I could do to make her feel at peace. We were short on time, and in my heart, I didn't want to see her die this way. I decided to write gratitude to her for each year of my life, created a playlist of songs to ease her tension, and compiled a list of her favorite bible scriptures to read.

The next day, I returned to the hospital, but the situation had worsened. Her health declined overnight, and the time had come to transition her to hospice for comfort care.

Once she arrived at hospice, the staff placed her on the board. My mother was agitated. The team told me she was yelling and was in a rage toward everyone. I felt defeated momentarily. My intention to bring her to a peaceful state was moving in the opposite direction. I walked into the room to check on her and she started screaming at me too. I began to pray for guidance. I walked away and thought I could shift her state. I went back into the room, slammed the door, got right in her face and said "The staff, me, and everyone is working around the clock to see to it that you are comfortable and you're yelling at all of us. What do you want?"

She looked at me in shock. It was the first time I stood up to her and yelled back. She looked at me and said, "I am waiting to go home to God." I gently told her God is and always has been with her. You never need to stay; you just need to surrender and let go. After I guided her through a mini meditation to calm her down, I started the playlist of songs, read every gratitude to her and recited her favorite bible verses. By this point, she was at peace. We exchanged some loving words with each other and I left. I knew in my heart my intention to transition her peacefully happened and she would pass within the next 48 hours.

The next day hospice called me and asked me about our visit as my mother had been calm and peaceful since. I smiled. I knew God gifted me my wish to have her transition peacefully. Shortly after, I received the call hours later that she had passed away. At this moment, I felt peace in my heart, and I knew it was her time, and I knew I truly forgave her for everything I thought she had ever done to me.

One of the greatest lessons I learned in my relationship with my mother is that we are all responsible for standing as a source in our world of who we desire to be by taking hundred percent responsibility for every event in our lives. The fear of disappointment and not being loved was released from my being and filled with love and deep compassion for my mom. I believe spending all those years doing the work of transforming myself helped my mother and I in her passing. I am deeply grateful for my mom, and I am thankful for everything she truly taught me to become the woman I am today. Everything in our lives is and always has been happening perfectly according to plan by divine design. Every wound holds wisdom…

"My scars remind that the damage
life has inflicted on me has,
in many places, left me stronger
and more resilient."

~ Steve Goodier

CHAPTER ELEVEN

---⋙∘⟨⟩∘⋘---

Pearls of Wisdom

By Cindy Vazquez

W hen I think of the many wounds I have accumulated through life, they feel heavy. Heavy to the point where I could never see those wounds as becoming tools to help me become wiser and brighter. I saw the wounds as oppressive and part of my culture and lifestyle. "Is there such a thing as wounds becoming wisdom?" This was the first question that came to mind when I was invited to co-author and share my experience of how my wounds have become wisdom. I pondered the question while listening to the invitation to become a co-author.

As a little Mexican-American girl, I loved the English Language. My first language was Spanish, which I learned from my parents. Spanish is a beautiful language but quite challenging to learn. So as a little girl, I pretended I knew English and would start speaking in weird sounds that mimicked English words and accents. According to my beautiful mother, I sounded funny and cute. I still remember the huge smile on my face while my mother was drying me after taking a shower. I loved seeing my mother enjoy my love for the English language. She would dry me, then dress me, and brush my hair while listening to my conversation in so-called English. Then, she would say to me, "One day, you will speak fluent English, and you will not remember a time in your life when you had no idea what you were saying."

The time arrived for the journey of my school years to be experienced. I remember being in a preschool classroom when I was just a toddler, when everything was fun, and it was always playtime. My mother eventually enrolled my brother and I into an elementary school in Mexico. She wanted us to keep our Spanish language and Mexican culture. My time in Mexican school was fun and educational. I began learning to read, write, add, subtract, multiply, and divide, but then my time in Mexican school ended after finishing 2nd grade. I was excited to learn that my mom had enrolled us in an elementary school in the USA! I told myself, "Finally, I'm going to learn how to speak, write, and read English!" I started 3rd grade in a beautiful school, all enclosing and refrigerated air conditioning in each classroom! This was amazing and a huge shock because I was used to Mexican schools where classrooms were not as modern or beautiful as this new USA elementary school my mother had enrolled us in.

The new elementary school was a step up from what I was used to. I remembered entering my classroom and seeing the desks with their chairs tucked in, and on top of the desks were piles of books. I started walking towards the tables to choose the desk I was going to sit in, but the top book had a name, so I thought this desk was taken. I kept walking towards other desks, and the same name I saw again on top of the book. I then realized it was the title of the book. Finally, I sat down but was afraid to touch the books because I had no idea that they were given to the students. I was used to my mom always having to buy our schoolbooks and school supplies. To me, touching the books without permission was stealing. So, I sat in my chair with my hands on top of my lap. Finally, our teacher welcomed us to the new school year and explained about the stack of books on top of the desk, but I didn't understand the words she was saying because I couldn't speak English. She eventually explained to me in Spanish that the pile of books was for me to use for the school year and to take care of them. I felt relieved.

We took a break to have recess and lunch, and I was thrilled with my new school, classroom, and teacher. I was looking forward to meeting new friends! I was in the cafeteria, ready to grab my lunch, when one of my classmates called me and started speaking English. I said to her in Spanish, "Sorry, I do not understand what you are saying. Can you tell me in Spanish?" She laughed and said I was an ignorant girl and a Juareña. Juareña is the name given to non-English speaking people from the Mexican city Juarez Chihuahua Mexico when they come to the border city of El Paso, Texas, USA.

I was discriminated against for not being fluent in English. I was shocked, devastated, and very sad to the point that I wanted to cry. This girl's attitude hurt my heart and self-esteem. I wished I could understand her and not have to go through this horrible feeling. I felt like I had cotton balls in my ears and couldn't understand what she was saying. This was my first wound, and it scarred me. I replied to her in Spanish that I did not appreciate her calling me Juareña, and one day, I was going to speak fluent English, and she would beg me to be her friend. I left, showing I was solid, and she didn't hurt me, but deep inside my heart, I was hurt. How can children so young be so cruel? All I wanted was to make new friends and learn the beautiful English language. I eventually learned how to speak, write, and read fluently in English, but this experience marked me for life, and my low self-esteem ruled my life.

On that day, I promised myself I would perfect my English so I would never again be wounded the way I was when I was in 3rd grade by my classmate.

Subconsciously, I carried this wound for years. I created a shield to protect myself from anyone who would attempt to discriminate against me for not speaking perfect English. I would be embarrassed to talk or to let anyone know I knew Spanish. My accent always gave me away, as well as the fact that I could speak Spanish. I would be asked why I hid that I knew two languages and was fluent in both. I would not explain the whole story, but I would share that I didn't want to be discriminated against again. Until one day, a good friend of mine asked me questions regarding my feelings of being embarrassed for being fluent in Spanish.

My friend told me, "The wound you carry from your childhood experience can be a positive tool in your life if you are open to understanding how it can help you become wise." My friend's advice got me thinking intensely. My brain asked how this wound could be a positive tool or even become a pearl of wisdom in my life. For example, if I continue to speak Spanish and do not continue to perfect my American accent, I will surely re-encounter discrimination or rejection.

The feeling of being rejected or discriminated against for not knowing a language is a horrible feeling that I do not wish on anyone. Still, because my friend said this childhood wound could be a positive tool, my mind was opened to a new perspective. For the past ten years, I have been working on my personal and spiritual growth, which has helped me understand the power of awareness and how our experiences are actually lessons that help us become wiser. One of the lessons I learned was not to take things personally and to ask myself why I took something personally or why the experience hurt me. This was a mechanism to help me recognize that my low self-esteem was not understanding the power granted to me by God. I am using God because I am a believer in God, who I know has blessed me with this amazing wisdom of love. He also gave me the gift of exploring this amazing life as a soul having the human experience.

The journey of personal and spiritual growth helped me understand the power of awareness but also the importance of lessons being tools to become wiser. This path also introduced me to the fact that we humans project ourselves onto others, but we just don't realize or understand in the moment of having the experience. I have learned the fact that when we project ourselves, we are reacting. Reactions can bring sour consequences. For example, in my case with my 3rd-grade classmate, I believed she was mean and cruel because she saw me as ignorant and lower than her just because I didn't understand or speak English. How could she be so inconsiderate and mean? As an adult who has learned to be aware of my power, I started to think, "maybe her parents had experienced discrimination and rejection. They must have passed this insecurity onto their child. How can an eight-year-old be inconsiderate to someone who didn't speak the language?"

I now understand that projection is a protection mechanism, a shield, which we adopt to protect ourselves from being hurt. I also see projection as judging. Judgment is a human condition which comes from ego, and it's a challenge to stop. When we judge, we are projecting. I am so grateful to spiritual growth for introducing and educating me in the art of compassion and empathy. Knowing I am judging brings the opportunity for me to start listening to the person who I perceive as projecting, and this also helps me understand that I could also be judging. Applying the art of listening minimizes my judgment and projection. Therefore, I understand where the other person is coming from. Otherwise, I would take it personally and defend myself. I understand it's wise to apply the art of listening and the art of empathy with compassion.

We all mirror each other in one way or another. This mirroring can be positive or negative. But it's all according to our perspective and awareness. I understand not to take anything personally, to ask questions, and to open a new way of thinking and feeling. Allowing me to question things and remain in a neutral state rather than a protective state has given me the wisdom to listen and have compassion toward others. Life is not always perfect, and we are here to learn, so sometimes, our ego will look to control our response depending on the situation. I now realize my fear of rejection and discrimination is part of my journey to understanding how we can turn around low self-esteem. We look to not go through hard times and stay in our comfort zone. Understand that the comfort zone is a safety zone, but no wisdom comes from the safety zone. We must be willing to step into the uncomfortable zone to continue growing and becoming wiser.

My mother always reminds me of my amazingness and often tells me I am a diamond in the process of being polished. She has been my teacher and reminds me of how wise and powerful I have become, especially when I go back and allow my old wounds and low self-esteem to rule my life. She reminds me of all my accomplishments and the courage I mustered to take action despite the fear and stress. Life is about the choices you make and proceed to act on. So, when I listen to my mother say I am a diamond, I tell myself in my mind while listening to her speak her magic words, "my mother sees with love and sees only beauty in me." My wounds have become wisdom for me to apply and continue this life with my head up.

My mother is correct. I am a diamond; I am polished but adding even more polish certainly doesn't hurt. This might sound funny, but we all are diamonds. We forget to see our power and amazingness. Our experiences are tools to not only help ourselves but to become an inspiration to others. My wounds aren't just there to continue to hurt me or make me a victim. These wounds are the wisdom to help others and guide those ready to understand their power and awareness. There are no negatives or positives, but lessons for us to learn and continue to grow.

One key factor is to understand that we aren't victims of our wounds. We are powerful beyond understanding. These wounds are a gift to embrace and be a light to oneself and others. How can you help, guide, and support if you don't go through these experiences? I often ask myself these questions. I am not going to lie; of course, I would rather be in my comfort zone, in my bubble where everything is safe, and no one will ever reject me or discriminate against me. I want to be in a place where I don't have to work on my low self-esteem, but how can that help me thrive? It's no help, especially when striving to continue to be better than yesterday. I continue to embrace the awareness that these are lessons and tools to help us in every moment of our lives.

Even though life is a journey and wounds will always be a part of our experience, our perspective changes when we become aware and understand that they are also pearls of wisdom. This reminds me of Dr. Wayne Dyer's (R.I.P.) quote, **"Change the way you look at things and the things you look at will change."** Our wounds are pearls of wisdom. We don't see them that way, especially when we are in the process of experiencing the wounds. How can we even think they are pearls of wisdom when they hurt so much? The power of awareness is magical, and the power of perspective is also powerful. We are beyond amazing, but we don't learn this from traditional teachings or our parents. We are taught that life is happening to us instead of for us. So, every time we become aware of life happening for us is when our wounds become our wisdom.

Embracing wounds as wisdom is a gift to brighten our lives and experiences. As I shared before, the fact that I was rejected and seen as less just for not speaking the English language didn't mean I *was* less, or I was being rejected. I was being projected on, and she was projecting her wounds, fears, and insecurities. I didn't know any better, and neither did she. So, I took it personally and allowed this situation to dim my power.

Personal growth, spiritual growth, and my friend, with her questions, opened my mind to a different perspective and feelings regarding my wounds being a scar on my life. I am grateful for my friend and her advice, which helped me revisit and question my childhood experiences. It opened my curiosity to explore more and understand how wounds become wisdom. My journey through personal growth and spiritual growth is a blessing. Understanding our power and awareness is key to seeking wisdom. Every moment counts. We will encounter experiences that could wound us, but they are lessons for us to continue exploring this amazing life. Embrace each moment, each wound but remember they are your tools to help you become wiser. You are the light of your journey, and with your light, you can become an inspiration to show others that there is a solution to our wounds.

"Dismantle your wounds so you stop living your life by them."

~ Nikki Rowe

CHAPTER TWELVE

Transcend your Wounds
By John Spender

These days, finding someone who doesn't know who Oprah Winfrey is would be difficult. The Oprah Winfrey Show, which ran for twenty-five seasons, was watched by millions daily. Oprah has been nominated for two Oscars, received dozens of awards, and was given the Presidential Medal of Freedom in 2013. She was the first Black American woman to own a production company, and today she is still heavily involved in the entertainment industry as an actress, producer, and powerhouse interviewer, scoring desirable sit-downs with personalities like Prince Harry and Meghan, Duchess of Sussex, Tom Cruise, and Whitney Houston, to name a few.

Today, her net worth is in the billions. But despite the picture of success and happiness that Oprah embodies today, life wasn't always perfect for the media titan. Much of Oprah's childhood was filled with trauma and abuse. So how did Oprah end up where she is today? Let's look at her childhood wounds and how she turned them into the wisdom that brought her success later in life - changing the lives of millions in the process.

> *"If you don't like something, change it. If you can't change it, change your attitude."*
> ~ Maya Angelou

Oprah was born to a young mother in Kosciusko, Mississippi. Although her family was poor, Oprah's grandmother, who raised her for the first six years of her life, was determined to provide her with a good education. She rigorously tutored the young toddler in reading, which resulted in her being bumped up a few grades once she entered school. However, while a good start to an education sounds positive enough, there is a darker side to Oprah's time with her grandmother. It's since been revealed that her grandmother used to beat Oprah so severely that she would bleed onto her clothes, which often resulted in another beating for getting her clothes dirty. However, despite the physical abuse and heavy expectations to perform well, it was the lesson of hard work that Oprah carried with her for the rest of her life. No matter how difficult that period of her life was, she saw the positives and took them with her on her journey.

Once she turned six, Oprah moved to Milwaukee to live with her mother and brothers. It was the beginning of several tumultuous years in Oprah's life, where her resilience would be tested again and again.

When Oprah arrived at her mother's house, she was instantly faced with something insidious: colorism and internalized racism. Although Oprah's mother was living with another Black woman, that woman had lighter skin and soon made it clear that she didn't wish to have Oprah set foot inside the house. So the six-year-old was actually forced to sleep outside on the porch that night, the very first night in a strange new place, away from the only home she had ever known.

Of course, anyone reading this story would rightfully be appalled. It would be understandable if Oprah had screamed, cried, or even run away from the house that night. But instead, she showed remarkable strength that night, and she turned to someone she knew would always be a friend to her: God. In interviews, she said she didn't feel alone that night because she had faith to keep her company.

"I don't remember ever shedding a tear about it because I knew that God was my father, Jesus was my brother, and they were with me."

What a remarkable moment. Here is a child who had every right to be terrified and angry, but instead turned her thinking towards what could give her comfort. She didn't place blame or anger anywhere but instead looked for inner peace—what an astounding way to take a wound and turn it into wisdom. Oprah would endure many more traumatic moments over the next few years.

At nine-years-old Oprah was sexually abused by one of her cousins, and over the next three years, she was subjected to repeated sexual abuse by several of her relatives. Without anyone intervening, all Oprah could do was survive, with only her thoughts to keep her company. She couldn't have known it at the time, but the abuse she suffered would later prompt her to help countless victims of sexual assault.

At fourteen, Oprah found herself pregnant because of the sexual abuse she had suffered. She gave birth to a premature baby boy, who died just weeks later in hospital.

Oprah's trauma by the age of fourteen was more than many will ever face in their lifetimes. So how could she have risen from such abuse and neglect to become one of the world's most positive and successful women?

First, she found an element of stability in her life: her father. She moved to her dad's place in Nashville, who soon made it clear that he had high expectations of his daughter. (Although unlike her grandmother, his expectations were not accompanied by harsh physical abuse.) He set firm rules surrounding her responsibilities and pushed her to dedicate herself to her studies. Once again, Oprah was reminded of the value of hard work, and in this more supportive environment, the young woman soon began to excel.

Oprah began acing her classes and winning awards for recitations. She was crowned Miss Black Tennessee at seventeen and started her first on-air television job at WVOL. She also received a full scholarship to study speech communications and performing arts at Tennessee State University. By her early twenties, she was working as a co-anchor and a reporter, and just ten years later, she was able to seize an opportunity to host the talk show that eventually became known as *The Oprah Winfrey Show.*

"From every wound, there is a scar, and every scar tells a story.
A story that says, 'I have survived.'"
~ Craig Scott

From there, many of us know the rest of the story. The show quickly rose to prominence, and led to countless awards and accolades over 25 years. What a transformation! Let's talk about how Oprah used the wounds she endured as a child and teenager to positively impact the world around her.

One principle that Oprah has stood by for many years is to "live your life from a place of truth." Although many of Oprah's past experiences are painful, and details of her childhood have been shared without her consent, Oprah knows that being truthful about her feelings and experiences is not only what has helped her heal, but is also what makes it possible for her to help others who may have gone through similar experiences.

The Oprah Winfrey Show aired more than 200 episodes that delved deep into the topic of sexual abuse. Oprah interviewed countless survivors and had many difficult conversations about domestic violence and even male sexual abuse victims.

Not only did Oprah's platform allow a place for victims to speak openly about their experiences, but it also opened the eyes of millions of viewers to the realities of sexual abuse. In speaking up about these horrific experiences, Oprah and her guests helped people around the world recognize the signs of abuse, which in turn helped many seek help, prevent, or sometimes even stop abuse from happening. Oprah knew that keeping her wounds private, it would only allow them to fester. By speaking candidly about her experiences and giving others a place to share theirs, she helped unthinkable numbers of people around the world. By telling her truth, Oprah turned her wounds into wisdom and helped destigmatize a subject that many had been too scared or uncomfortable to discuss.

"You see, there is no darker secret than sexual abuse. I am telling you about myself, so maybe the closet where many sexual abuse victims and their abusers hide might swing open just a crack today and let some light in."

Nothing can change what happened to Oprah as a child; undoubtedly, she experiences her fair share of anger and sadness when she remembers the wrongs committed against her. But she found the positive in an impossible situation by using her past to help others, and there can be nothing more healing.

Another way that Oprah has learned to turn her wounds into wisdom is by practicing gratefulness. Every day Oprah writes down what she is grateful for, and it has made her appreciate everything she has in life, even when it would have been easy to feel like she didn't have much to be thankful for in life. In a commencement speech at Wellesley College in 1997, she said: *"If you concentrate and focus in your life on what you don't have, you will never have enough. Be grateful. Keep a journal."*

What empowering words of wisdom. Remember, these are words from a woman who grew up in poverty and endured years of physical and sexual abuse at the hands of her family. It would have been easy for her to be bitter and resentful, but instead of dwelling on the bad parts of her life, she learned to practice gratitude and spent more energy focusing on the good parts. This shows how powerful our thoughts and responses to negative situations can change our outcomes.

Sadly, many people can identify closely with Oprah's story, and it might not be easy to overcome anger, sadness, and the trauma of your abuse. Still, it's a worthy goal to make peace with your past by talking about it to liberate yourself and others. Her life demonstrates how powerful our minds are, and that we can turn our wounds into something extraordinary.

Like Oprah, I'm one of the millions worldwide who has endured sexual and physical abuse at my family's hands. You wouldn't wish it on anyone, but there is a gift in the adversity we all go through on some level with this journey called life. I had suppressed what had happened to me for decades, building a brick wall around my wounded child because I believed that was the safest thing to do. But, unfortunately, I now know this was the worst thing you could do. I had created secrets, and my unloved parts began to rot within the prison I had built. They later festered into drug and alcohol abuse as a negative coping mechanism for my untreated trauma.

I didn't learn how to read and write at a basic level until I was ten in a developed country like Australia. The shame I carried about my learning capabilities as a child haunted me for many years afterward. Facing my life through counseling, healing sessions with a Reiki healer and attending seminars enabled me to open up and cry. This was a positive step towards healing my past.

Writing about my experiences of emotional, physical and sexual abuse, although extremely confronting, was profoundly healing. It's challenging for many reasons, but the three that stand out the most are facing the pain of the events and reliving it, the fear of backlash from family, and the dread of being judged. These heavy emotions can be too much for many to defy. It took me years to conciliate my wounds from childhood to the point where I'm at peace with them. I'm not sure if wounds ever fully heal. I feel that we learn to become okay with them until they develop scar tissue that becomes softer over time.

If I could relive my journey, I wouldn't suffer so much over what was done to me. It wastes time and energy in anger, hurt and resentment. There's a common question that many interviewers ask: "What would your future self tell the younger version of you?" I'd tell my younger self to move as quickly as possible to focus on healing your trauma rather than where it came from or who caused it. Buddha says, "If you get hit with an arrow, it's more important to treat the wound than worry about where the arrow came from or who fired it." How you feel about this statement tells you if you are still stuck in the wound, ready to transform it into wisdom, or have some insights of your own to share. Which one are you?

> *"The secret of change is to focus all your energy,*
> *not on fighting the old, but on building the new."*
> ~ Dan Millman

I was a life coach for seven years before becoming a book publisher, after which I volunteered for three months at mission Australia in Sydney. I have heard many childhood horror stories and even published a few. Periods in our life can and will be challenging, but things don't have to be all bad. I think sometimes we allow the negative times in our life to cloud the positive things happening all around us. There is a scene in *The Way of the Peaceful Warrior* when Nick Nolte's character Socrates grabs his student, bringing him into the present moment and showing all the magical moments happening simultaneously. He states that there is nothing never going on. The question is, are you awake to reality? At any given moment, we have good and bad things happening, and our focus determines our reality. Like Oprah, we can transform the negative aspects of our life into blessings that benefit both us and the world.

Another lesson we can glean from Oprah's incredible life story is that after many bad experiences, she learned, *"When people show you who they are the first time, believe them."* By trusting her instincts and accepting that some people would continually let her down, Oprah could surround herself with people she knew would support and love her because they have made that evident from the beginning. That can be a harsh lesson to learn, especially when you care about someone, but realizing that someone who lets you down once will let you down again will help weed out the people who aren't going to be able to let you live your best life.

> *"Turn your hurt into healing, your wounds into wisdom and your pain into power."*
> ~ Robin Sharma

Of course, all wounds need healing. You must seek help and support for the trauma that has happened to you, but remember that you can also use your wounds to transform your life for the greater good. Now I invite you to review the wisdom that Oprah has blessed us with.

1. Live in your truth
   Be open about who you are and the experiences you've had. Only by doing so can you move through your trauma and find the wisdom on the other side.

2. Have faith
   Oprah is a Christian, but you can have faith in whatever god or belief works for you. Knowing that someone or something is on your side and things will eventually work out for you is a powerful belief.

3. Practice gratitude
   Oprah encourages everyone to keep a journal and write at least five things they're grateful for daily. Only by practic-

ing gratitude can you truly see how much abundance you have in your life.

4. When someone shows you who they are the first time, believe them. When someone waves a red flag, pay attention. Don't push aside that voice in the back of your head; instead, surround yourself with people who inspire and support you.

5. Work hard
No matter your circumstances, hard work will eventually pay off; somewhere, somehow, what we put into the world will return to us.

How can you follow Oprah's five lessons for transforming your wounds into wisdom?

Often we can feel like life is happening to us rather than for us. Life is simply mirroring back to us our most dominant thoughts and emotions. I learned a valuable lesson when I was 16. I used to self-harm with cuts and burns; a group of us at school used to do this from time to time. As stupid as it is, I now see the pain that we were suppressing. One of the ways we would encourage each other to self-harm was called a smiley. You heat a lighter and burn it into your arm, leaving a smiley face.

I was at a friend's place (let's call him Sam) one afternoon, and we were doing smileys. Sam wanted to give me a smiley and said the lighter was hot and that he didn't think I could handle it. His brother helped by holding my arm steady as Sam melted the lighter into my arm, making a hissing sound as he did so. It was painful and the blister was huge, but being tough was considered cool, so I put on a brave face and dealt with it. I still have the scar from that afternoon today. When I look at it, it reminds me of how much pain I was in back then. It fuels my motivation to work on myself even more. Luckily my self-harming days are over and I surround myself with good people who only want the best for me. I've learned to forgive myself and others, and to create my best life. Shortly after that smiley incident, I was accepted into a horticultural college program. I dedicated myself to my studies, which led me to start my first Landscaping business, and a healthier direction in life.

> *"If we are to nurture and heal, we must*
> *admit that the wounds exist."*
> ~ Iyanla Vanzant

I discovered that when we peel back the layers of our wounds, we simultaneously gain access to the wisdom from that experience. The value I have received from being part of various group coaching programs has been immense. Having someone facilitate group exercises and content designed to uncover and heal your wounds is powerful. Often this is the only way to move through them, as they are too much of a burden to carry ourselves. It takes courage and a willingness to show up for our transformation before we can action the wisdom we gain from such processes. One of the best ways is in a group; people are designed to help and support each other along the way. When we help someone else, we instantly feel good about raising our self-esteem from the act.

By focusing and practicing our responsibility to self-improvement, we make ourselves and the world a better place. Of course, it won't always be easy, but you should know that there are many support groups, both free and paid, that can assist you in transforming your wounds into wisdom. I encourage you to take steps to advance towards your dreams and faith in the world. Know that success leaves clues left by people like Oprah Winfrey, teaching us that step-by-step, anything is possible.

"Wounds ain't obstruction, wounds are wind for the sails of your lifeboat."

~ Abhijit Naskar

AUTHOR BIOGRAPHIES

Dr. Olga Zabora

CHAPTER ONE

Dr. Olga Zabora, Certified Master NLP Coach and NLP Trainer's Trainer holds a Doctorate Degree in Clinical Psychology from the US, Diploma of Clinical Hypnotherapy from HMI and multiple certifications including Gestalt Therapy at PGI and Jungian Analytical Psychology at Jung Institute of Los Angeles, Past Life Regression & Spiritual Regression w/ Brian Weiss.

Her extensive training both in the US and outside the country combined with 20 years of education and experience allows for forward thinking and advanced knowledge and flexibility, love for life and people, helpful in creating transformational changes in your life.

Her personal far-reaching experiences and deep exploration of Jungian Therapy, Dream Analysis, Holotropic Breathwork® with Stan Grof, meditation, mindfulness, yoga, philosophical tantra, sacred temple mandala dance in India, multiple studies about feminine nature and energy from world renown professionals.

Certificate from Optimum Health Institute and Advanced Nutritional and Integrative Medicine for Mental Health Professionals,

Shamanism from Michael Harner's Foundation, and other spiritual practices has given the opportunities to integrate her knowledge and utilize it in assisting clients with their life journeys and lasting positive changes.

Her passion lies in helping you become aware of your own resources by bringing up the best parts of yourself to guide you gently with your conscious transformation into the best and happiest version of yourself.

Currently Olga is publishing her books, continuing clinical practice, coaching, teaching classes and conducting empowering women's retreats along with sharing her humor, knowledge and experience with everyone who attends her courses at www. GoddessEvent.com

Bec Bucci
CHAPTER TWO

Rebecca (Bec) Bucci is an American Board Certified Sexologist, Clinical Sexuality Coach, Global Speaker and Relationships Sexpert.

Founder of G Spot Sex Therapy Down Under, her work specialises in educating couples and individuals in all areas of taboo, sexual dysfunction and rehabilitation. Her passionate approach of inspiring women to embrace their complete sexual self and in expressing their deepest desires around pleasure have led her to be featured in international best selling print magazines and international best selling books as a featured Coauthor.

Rebecca facilitates couples, women and men's workshops and retreats globally via face to face instruction and via the G Spot online subscription app.

Rebecca states "Becoming a Sexologist was my calling, my life's work, to open the door to acceptance of the weird, of the taboo, of the kink, of the extra-ordinary expressions we can experience whilst living through this human experience. This is my purpose to inspire all women to step fully into their femininity "now," to embrace it, allowing it to ignite by trusting it and finally by nurturing it through its many stages of maturity. ALWAYS tend to the fire within. Don't wait to become…

An unapologetically, authentically raw and real 100% woman."

Lyn Croker

CHAPTER THREE

Lyn Croker- Superwoman vs Realwoman

Relationship coach, Positive Psychology coach.

Lyn's motto is "Relationships don't have to be that hard."

If you're feeling:

- Disconnected with your partner
- Unappreciated and unloved
- Confused - do you stay or go?
- Tired of fighting and shutting down
- Don't know what makes you happy any more

Lyn's workshops and programs will help:

- Reignite your passion
- Improve your intimacy
- Discover communication tools to eliminate misunderstandings/miscommunication

- Understand your partners feelings and how to respond not react
- Learn how to set boundaries
- Fall back in love
- Get clarity around your fears
- Feel more understood, seen, appreciated and loved
- Be more comfortable with speaking your truth

When you have some basic strategies/tools to help you understand yourself and your partner, that you can implement immediately, it will help you **fall back in love with each other.**

Lyn has travelled the World for 30+ years speaking, coaching, and learning about relationships, and human behaviour. She is an international best selling author, former paramedic, mother of eight children, and wife.

If any of this resonates with you then contact Lyn for a chat

Contact details:

Lyn Croker

Ph 61 0602 254 042

Email: lyn@superwomanvsrealwoman.com

Website: https://www.superwomanvsrealwoman.com/

Facebook: https://www.facebook.com/superwomanvsrealwoman

Linkedin: https://www.linkedin.com/in/lynelliott

Amita McBride
CHAPTER FOUR

Amita McBride is a gifted intuitive and pioneer who works with people, animals and the earth, helping to facilitate deep transformation and healing in all aspects of life.

She has a passion to create the extraordinary, personally doing so through her own ongoing awakening. Amita created her Sacred Raw Cacao healing line working with the grandmother plants to open, balance and strengthen the body, mind and spirit.

Amita's work is founded upon personal empowerment to one's path of the heart, helping people align with new paradigms of belief, healing and expansion. She bridges diverse similarities and life's interconnectedness through her visionary approach.

She assists both people and animals on their journey within. Love is the cornerstone for all change. Amita has written two books and is currently working on a new one. She resides in Montana. For more information about her offerings, please visit her website: rideswithfire.com.

Joanne Colely

CHAPTER FIVE

Spending 20 years working in the corporate world of Yellow Pages and Google, a life changing event caused her to throw it all away and start all over again by following her dream of teaching art. However, halfway through her teaching degree, she decided to pursue painting celebrities and politicians to help raise money for charity.

After she painted at her first ever event (using only her hands and fingers) painting giant mermaids swimming underneath Rottnest island which raised $52,000, she became quite popular!

Since then, she has gone on to paint the former Prime Minister Scott Morrison, Mark McGowan, Daniel Ricciardo, Nat Fyfe, Nic Naitanui, Ray Meager (Alf Stewart from Home and Away,) Damian Martin, Bryce Cotton, Basil Zempilas, Anthony Mundine and Dr Charlie Teo raising just under $200,000 so far. More recently, she has been asked to paint the Duchess of York Sarah Ferguson.

Her main focus now is painting commissions and selling her collection of works where her style is extremely diverse. Painting from landscapes to portraits, to a surrealist narrative collection of works and more recently large glass resin pieces.

Some of her works are held by private collectors both nationally and internationally. Next year she will be exhibiting internationally in Poland and in Ireland. In 2023, she will be walking the TEDX stage to tell her story of her art journey to inspire others that with the right mindset, they can follow their dreams.

Please see Joanne Colely's website to view her work and to see her foxtel interviews and to look at her latest adventures on www. joannecolely.com.au

Catherine Schwark
CHAPTER SIX

Catherine is a Master Integrative Life Coach and is the Founder and CEO of CAT Coaching: *Conscious Action Transformations.* She is certified by the Instinctual Trauma Response Training Institute; is a member of Tony Robbin's Inner Circle; and is a Founding Member of The Recovery Church in St. Paul, MN.

In her book, *Enough!! From Self-Sabotage to Self-Empowerment* she instills clarity, confidence and courage in the reader's personal development through education, empowerment and engagement. She includes stories from her own life, the lessons and practices she's learned, and a reader's reflection that inspires the reader to take action for change in their own lives. It is scheduled for release in early 2023.

She also offers a *Enough! From Self-Sabotage to Self-Empowerment* self-paced 12-week coaching program that assists her clients in discovering and moving from their own self-sabotaging behaviors to taking control of their lives and to stand strong and claim self-empowerment. Individual coaching may also be available.

She is dedicated to a Seven Generational stewardship to leave an impactful, inspiring, and illuminating family and community legacy that impresses a positive influence into the future regarding health, wealth, love and connection.

She lives in Minnesota, USA and can be reached at MNCatherine11@gmail.com and followed or messaged at: https://www.facebook.com/MNCatherine

Nadia Elmagrabi
CHAPTER SEVEN

Nadia Elmagrabi MA is a Psychotherapy-Informed Intuitive Guide specializing in Past Life Therapy. Nadia holds impeccable space for women (& men) to confront the deepest and darkest places within themselves.

She has an uncanny ability to guide her clients where they need to go to heal what they need to heal, so they can move forward in their lives, be aligned with their higher self, and express their fullest potential.

As well as Past Life Therapy, Nadia incorporates Soul Realignment, Human Design, Shamanic Healing sessions, and a variety of other modalities into her work with clients so that by the time their work together is complete, her clients feel transformed from the person they once were.

They no longer experience debilitating anxiety and depression, they feel renewed and refreshed, their relationships improve, and they are clear on who they are, what they want, and where they are going.

Nadia is married to her Soulmate, and together they have two brilliant boys and their dog, Tazo.

You can learn more about Nadia and connect with her here:

Website: www.NadiaElmagrabi.com

Facebook: https://www.facebook.com/n.elmagrabi

Instagram: https://www.instagram.com/nadia_elmagrabi/

Email: NadiaElmagrabi@gmail.com

Maria Loper
CHAPTER EIGHT

Maria Loper is originally from Christchurch, New Zealand and has been working in the community sector in both New Zealand and Australia since the 1990s and in the mental health sector for the last eight years, as a Team Leader/ Mental Health Recovery Worker for a local NGO in Ipswich, Brisbane.

This is Maria's first memoir writing project and for her this has been an amazingly creative way for her to express herself more fully and authentically.

In this chapter she gives you a glimpse into her harrowing experiences whilst in the middle of town at the epicentre of the Christchurch Earthquakes in 2011.

Maria let's you into her world as she explains how this event was a catalyst that became a very transformative and healing process for her. Maria then explores the deeper meanings of life, who she is, what she loves and how she would like to live her life more fully as she moves forward.

Maria's intention in writing this chapter was to inspire you to realise that transformation, healing and hope are always possible no matter what you go through in life.

Jenny Bot
CHAPTER NINE

Jenny AKA Botlady on twitch, collaborating with an international gaming community, is always aspiring to connect with new people. She is especially interested in spiritual growth and wellness, studying with many healers throughout her life. Her three small children are her greatest joy in life, and inspiration to make the world a better place.

Join along in her story starting in the early 1980s, growing up in an idyllic childhood in a San Francisco California suburb. Jenny suffered through the pain of a car accident in her late teens, to a semester in Italy's nightclubs during college in her early 20s.

She is all about personal growth and is a lifelong learner, graduating with her Bachelorette in Biology and most interested in global issues and the environment. Jenny struggled to find stability in her personal relationships, but never lost her passion for living life. She lived through the suicides of both her father and husband just three months apart in 2016. Find out how she was able to overcome PTSD and find herself again.

Jenny strives to inspire others to never give up on their hopes and dreams.

She now resides in California, you might find her doing yoga in her garden with her second husband and three children.

You can reach out to her by Twitter: @botlady4

Sonja Anastasia
CHAPTER TEN

Sonja Anastasia resides in New York. She is a former financial services professional, for 17 years. She decided two years ago to follow her passionate heart's desire into coaching women.

She is certified as a life & business coach, meditation instructor, NLP, sound therapy, and various leadership trainings. Her holistic approach to coaching brings clarity, grounding, direction, alignment and positive support to empower woman to heal within, reclaim their lives, and expand their magic.

Sonja also helps her clients find their own voice, true heart's desires by bridging the gaps between their past life experience into the present; and go to where they like to be.

She truly believes we all have a shining bright light within us bursting to come forth. All we need to do together is clear our energy, shift our beliefs, create new ways of being; one step at a time to capture our radiant essence residing within us all along. In her free time Sonja loves travelling, art, cooking, hiking and photography.

Cindy Vazquez
CHAPTER ELEVEN

Cindy is a loving free spirited women who loves to explore and go on adventures. Even though she loves to explore and welcomes most adventures, she still has fears and would rather stay in the comfort safe zone. Cindy knows and understands that the comfort zone is where growth is delayed or gets stagnant. One of her many attributes is her strong will to continue striving to become better than what she was before. Her focus now in this stage of her life is to be a walking example to her adorable son, her family, friends, and those she meets along the way.

Cindy was born in the land of the free, the USA, from immigrant parents. Thanks to her parent's courage and will to move to a new country and provide for her brother and her, she is able to pay it forward, not only to her family, but to those around her and society.

Cindy is a wife and a military wife. She always supports her husband and soldier with support and understanding that military life brings challenging situations, but are not impossible to fulfill! She is a strong women who is also compassionate and loving. She is passionate, and her passion pushes and motivates her to take action to always be a tool for God's given gift of sovereignty and natural freedoms! She is courageous, and her courage is what keeps her in action to continue progressing in life.

John Spender
CHAPTER TWELVE

John Spender is a 29-time International Best Selling co-author, who didn't learn how to read and write at a basic level until he was ten-years-old. He has since traveled to more than 65 countries, territories and started many businesses leading him to create the best-selling book series *A Journey Of Riches*. He is an Award Winning International Speaker and Movie Maker.

John worked as an international NLP trainer and coached thousands of people from various backgrounds through many challenges. From the borderline homeless to wealthy individuals, he has helped many people connect with their truth to create a life on their terms.

John's search for answers to living a fulfilling life has taken him to work with Native American Indians in the Hills of San Diego, to the forests of Madagascar, swimming with humpback whales in Tonga, exploring the Okavango Delta of Botswana and climbing the Great Wall of China. He's traveled from Chile to Slovakia, Hungary to the Solomon Islands, the mountains of Italy and the streets of Mexico.

Everywhere his journey has taken him, John has discovered a hunger among people to find a new way to live, with a yearning for freedom of expression. His belief that everyone has a book in them was born.

He is now a writing coach, having worked with over 400 authors from 40 countries for the *A Journey of Riches* series http://ajourneyofriches.com/ and his publishing house, Motion Media International, has published 31 non-fiction titles to date.

John also co-wrote and produced the movie documentary *Adversity* starring Jack Canfield, Rev. Micheal Bernard Beckwith, Dr. John Demartini and many more, coming soon in 2022. And you can bet there will be a best-selling book to follow!

AFTERWORD

I hope you enjoyed the collection of heartfelt stories, wisdom and vulnerability shared. Storytelling is the oldest form of communication, and I hope you feel inspired to take a step toward living a fulfilling life. Feel free to contact any of the authors in this book or the other books in this series.

The proceeds of this book will feed many of the rural Balinese families that are struggling.

Other books in the series are...

Motivate Your Life: A Journey of Riches, Book Twenty Nine
https://www.amazon.com/dp/B0BCXMF11P

Awaken to Your Inner Truth: A Journey of Riches, Book Twenty Eight
https://www.amazon.com/dp/B09YLYMQ4H?geniuslink=true

Awaken to Your Inner Truth: A Journey of Riches, Book Twenty Eight
https://www.amazon.com/dp/B09YLYMQ4H?geniuslink=true

The Power of Inspiration: A Journey of Riches, Book Twenty Seven
http://mybook.to/ThePowerofInspiration

Messages from The Heart: A Journey of Riches, Book Twenty Six
http://mybook.to/MessagesOfHeart

Abundant living: A Journey of Riches, Book Twenty Five
https://www.amazon.com/dp/B0963N6B2C

The Way of the Leader: A Journey of Riches, Book Twenty Four
https://www.amazon.com/dp/1925919285

The Attitude of Gratitude: A Journey of Riches, Book Twenty Three
https://www.amazon.com/dp/1925919269

Facing your Fears: A Journey of Riches, Book Twenty Two
https://www.amazon.com/dp/1925919218

Returning to Love: A Journey of Riches, Book Twenty One
https://www.amazon.com/dp/B08C54M2RB

Develop Inner Strength: A Journey of Riches, Book Twenty
https://www.amazon.com/dp/1925919153

Building your Dreams: A Journey of Riches, Book Nineteen
https://www.amazon.com/dp/B081KZCN5R

Liberate your Struggles: A Journey of Riches, Book Eighteen
https://www.amazon.com/dp/1925919099

In Search of Happiness: A Journey of Riches, Book Seventeen
https://www.amazon.com/dp/B07R8HMP3K

Tapping into Courage: A Journey of Riches, Book Sixteen
https://www.amazon.com/dp/B07NDCY1KY

The Power Healing: A Journey of Riches, Book Fifteen
https://www.amazon.com/dp/B07LGRJQ2S

The Way of the Entrepreneur: A Journey Of Riches, Book Fourteen
https://www.amazon.com/dp/B07KNHYR8V

Discovering Love and Gratitude: A Journey Of Riches, Book Thirteen
https://www.amazon.com/dp/B07H23Q6D1

Transformational Change: A Journey Of Riches, Book Twelve
https://www.amazon.com/dp/B07FYHMQRS

Finding Inspiration: A Journey Of Riches, Book Eleven
https://www.amazon.com/dp/B07F1LS1ZW

Building your Life from Rock Bottom: A Journey Of Riches, Book Ten
https://www.amazon.com/dp/B07CZK155Z

Transformation Calling: A Journey Of Riches, Book Nine
https://www.amazon.com/dp/B07BWQY9FB

Letting Go and Embracing the New: A Journey Of Riches, Book Eight
https://www.amazon.com/dp/B079ZKT2C2

Making Empowering Choices: A Journey Of Riches, Book Seven
https://www.amazon.com/Making-Empowering-Choices-Journey-Riches-ebook/dp/B078JXMK5V

The Benefit of Challenge: A Journey Of Riches, Book Six
https://www.amazon.com/dp/B0778S2VBD

Personal Changes: A Journey Of Riches, Book Five
https://www.amazon.com/dp/B075WCQM4N

Dealing with Changes in Life: A Journey Of Riches, Book Four
https://www.amazon.com/dp/B0716RDKK7

Making Changes: A Journey Of Riches, Book Three
https://www.amazon.com/dp/B01MYWNI5A

The Gift In Challenge: A Journey Of Riches, Book Two
https://www.amazon.com/dp/B01GBEML4G

From Darkness into the Light: A Journey Of Riches, Book One
https://www.amazon.com/dp/B018QMPHJW

Thank you to all the authors who have shared aspects of their lives, hoping to inspire others to live a bigger version of themselves.

I want to share a beautiful quote from the great Jim Rohan, "You can't complain and feel grateful at the same time." At any given moment, we have a choice to either feel like a victim of life or be connected and grateful for it. I hope this book helps you feel grateful and inspires you to go after your dreams.

For more information about contributing to the series, visit http://ajourneyofriches.com/. Furthermore, if you enjoyed reading this book, we would appreciate your review on Amazon to help get our message out to even more readers.

Made in United States
North Haven, CT
17 December 2022